arth Dances

Music in Search of the Primitive

ANDREW FORD

'Andrew [Ford] demonstrates that our species' original sonic impulses echo down through the millennia, only to reorder themselves in chameleonic fashion and erupt everywhere from the disco to the opera hall.'
—**Brian Ritchie, Violent Femmes**

Andrew Ford uncovers the fascinating ways in which music and primitivism intersect. A dazzling and original journey through culture, *Earth Dances* unpicks our musical timeline from Beethoven to Elvis's hips, *The Rite of Spring* to the Sex Pistols.

Alternating between chapters of criticism and interviews with musical greats

ISBN: 978-1-86395-712-0 • RRP $29.99

February 2015 Release • 240 pages

...singers. Acclaimed author and broadcaster Andrew Ford explores the relationship between primal forms of music and the most refined examples of the art—'Too much refinement can obscure the emotional thrust of a work of art; dazzled by its surface, we fail to to attend to the real content of a painting or poem or piece of music.'

Ford highlights the constant flux of music, revealing the composers who dared to strip away bad habits and tired thinking in pursuit of new energy and ideas.

ANDREW FORD is the author of *Try Whistling This*, *Illegal Harmonies* and *The Sound of Pictures*. He is a composer, writer and broadcaster and presents The Music Show on ABC Radio National. His awards include the Paul Lowin Prize for his song cycle *Learning to Howl*, a Green Room Award for his opera *Rembrandt's Wife*, and the Geraldine Pascall Prize for critical writing. In 2009 he was resident composer at the Australian National Academy of Music.

For more information please contact Imogen Kandel on
03 9486 0288 / 0402 377 360 or imogen@blackincbooks.com

EMBARGO:
Monday 2 February 2015

Black Inc.
37–39 Langridge Street, Collingwood VIC 3066 Australia
tel: 03 9486 0288 / fax: 03 9486 0244
http://www.blackincbooks.com
facebook.com/blackincbooks @BlackincBooks

Black Inc. is an imprint of Schwartz Media Pty Ltd ABN 75 748 797 539

EARTH DANCES

MUSIC IN SEARCH OF THE PRIMITIVE

ANDREW FORD

Black Inc.

Published by Black Inc.,
an imprint of Schwartz Publishing Pty Ltd
37–39 Langridge Street
Collingwood VIC 3066 Australia
email: enquiries@blackincbooks.com
www.blackincbooks.com

Copyright © Andrew Ford 2015
Andrew Ford asserts his right to be known as the author of this work.

ALL RIGHTS RESERVED.
No part of this publication may be reproduced, stored in a retrieval system, or transmitted
in any form by any means electronic, mechanical, photocopying, recording or otherwise
without the prior consent of the publishers.

The National Library of Australia Cataloguing-in-Publication entry:

Ford, Andrew, 1957– author.
Earth dances: music in search of the primitive / Andrew Ford.
9781863957120 (paperback)
9781925203011 (ebook)
Musical analysis. Music and dance. Primitivism.
781

Cover design by Peter Long
Cover artwork: Freely modified from one of the forty-four drawings
from the portfolio *Le Tumulte Noir*, published by Paul Colin in 1927.
© Paul Colin/ADAGP. Licensed by Viscopy, 2014.
Internal design by Thomas Deverall

Printed in Australia by Griffin Press. The paper this book is printed
on is certified against the Forest Stewardship Council® Standards.
Griffin Press holds FSC chain of custody certification SGS-
COC-005088. FSC promotes environmentally responsible, socially
beneficial and economically viable management of the world's forests.

to the memory of
Wilfrid Mellers

CONTENTS

It is practically the only question of the age, this question of primitivism and how it can be sustained in the face of sophistication.

—JEAN RENOIR, 1968

The Primitive Urge

There is a moment, just before the end of Elliott Carter's *A Symphony of Three Orchestras* (1975), where things fall apart. Prior to it, we have experienced one of the composer's high-velocity rides, the music wheeling and soaring around three large groups of instruments in thirteen minutes of virtuosity, colour, subtlety, and rhythmic and metrical complexity. The texture abruptly thins out to a lyrical solo violin, then there is a loud crash and everything stops. A vain effort to start up again is silenced by a second crash, more brutal than the first. A second, more tentative attempt. Another crash. Then nothing. Then another crash and the whole orchestra is back, brass heavy and pounding away, but it quickly exhausts itself. Another silence, another crash.

We have no idea what will happen next. Finally, following failed attempts by various instruments to activate simple repeating figures, the piece peters out. It's an electrifying three minutes to which you feel all of Carter's previous music had been leading, as multiple flights of fancy are brought, with a bang, down to earth.

All music is a synthesis of intellectual design and bodily urge. Some is almost entirely the former and some the latter, but both impulses are necessary to a degree. Throughout history, music has required this sort of balance. The human soul (for want of a better word) cannot make do with dancing alone: it will inevitably go off in search of more fantastic musical designs, more complex patterns, more rarefied sounds. But equally, when the intellect dominates for too long, we listen out for music we can tap our feet to, something we can go home humming, or just some good, loud bangs as at the end of *A Symphony of Three Orchestras*.

It is hard to be at all precise about the motivation for different types of music. There was a time in Europe – up to the Renaissance and even beyond – when most complex music was commissioned by the church and composed for the liturgy. Secular music was songs and dances. There, you might think, is our dichotomy on a plate. But immediately we run up against exceptions. For example, a secular song such as 'Mon fin est ma commencement' by Guillaume de Machaut (c. 1300–77) contains rhythmic and contrapuntal complexity in the service of the ingenious formal design described in its title: it is a double palindrome, so the song's end is indeed its beginning. On the other hand, while the *Missa L'homme armé* by Guillaume Dufay (c. 1397–1474) lacks for nothing in complexity, this famous early-Renaissance Mass is based on a popular song of the day. Indeed, it is one of dozens of Mass settings which took this tune as their basis.

When composers have sought to make their music more authentic, they have generally done so by simplifying it – harmonically or rhythmically or texturally – or by making it less varied, by keeping a pattern going on and on. They have done it by making the pulse or beat of the music clearer so that it can be danced to. They have made the sound of their music more raw, less cooked, to use Claude Lévi-Strauss's distinction. They have drawn on folk music or popular songs or dances in the hope of bringing a new atmosphere or colour or vigour to their work. They have aimed for the primitive.

In polite society we tend to avoid this word 'primitive'. When discussing culture or international politics, the term always feels loaded and often pejorative. While in some areas of life – plumbing, for example – primitive is definitely not good, mostly its meaning is less cut and dried, and we are careful how we bandy the word about.

Once, the industrialised West spoke of 'primitive peoples'. Then it was 'backward nations', then 'under-developed nations', then we settled on 'developing nations'. I believe the current term is 'less economically developed countries'. This was never simply a matter of trying not to give offence; it was also about accuracy. The countries variously labelled 'backward' and 'under-developed' were only ever those things in relation to modern technological economies. Even then, the assumption that it was better to be a thriving industrial nation than, say, a nomadic people was debatable. In poetry or painting – or, for that matter, farming – some of these 'primitive' peoples might have been able to teach the 'developed' countries a thing or two about imagination and technique, let alone sustainability. The term 'less economically developed' still assumes there is only one way forward, one sort of progress, but it is more accurate than the other descriptors.

The word 'primitive' really means *first*, and specifically it refers to the first age or the first time. By extension, it may be used to denote something or someone with primitive qualities. But what are those qualities? And what are artists hoping to gain when they admit 'primitive' influences to their work?

Some artists have felt that embracing folkloric influences, for instance, helps to anchor their work in human experience, in reality. But it is also true that artists have simply adopted what they have taken to be a primitive ethos, simplifying their work, roughing it up, painting with broader strokes, dancing with heavier feet, singing and playing with more insistent rhythms. The *Oxford English Dictionary* gives, as equivalents of 'primitive', 'simple, rude or rough', and it is in these senses that I will mostly use the word in this book, because the book's principal subject is why skilled, trained, sophisticated musicians should want their music to sound or to be primitive. Why did Carter wish to derail his symphony? Why did he replace the rhythmic flexibility of the first part of his piece with loud bangs and simple repetition?

The English musicologist and composer Wilfrid Mellers (1914–2008) distinguished between 'corporeal rhythm' and 'spiritual rhythm'. For him, the former comes from or is related to the body – it is rhythm we can feel, that we tap our feet to, that we are tempted to dance to – while the latter is a rhythm of the mind, rhythm that we count. In making this distinction, Mellers was doubtless drawing on the American composer and instrument inventor Harry Partch (1901–74), who had spoken of 'corporeal music' and 'abstract music'.

Partch was being more specific than Mellers, for what he meant by 'corporeal music' was a performance that involved the whole body, that made no distinction, for instance, between sound and movement, music and theatre, musicians and dancers, and that was capable of embracing the everyday. In many of his pieces, Partch included a speaking voice (generally his own) reciting texts either from literary sources such as James Joyce or Lewis Carroll, or, more strikingly, from the world around him. In *Barstow* (1941–67), for example, we hear words collected from graffiti inscribed by Depression-era hobos, alternately spoken and chanted in a folk-like (at least, non-classical) manner. These voices, in tandem with the sounds of self-invented percussion instruments, now plunking, now scurrying, mark out Partch's *Barstow* as an example of what Daniel Albright called 'the modernist urge to restore corporeality to art'.

Albright was correct that this was a 'modernist urge', but it was also about balance. Mellers's distinction between 'corporeal' and 'spiritual' rhythm defines a dichotomy that is an important aspect of this balance. There is some music that is almost entirely 'corporeal' – 'drum and bass', for instance. Other music is, to all intents and purposes, wholly 'spiritual' – one thinks of *The Art of Fugue*, which some people believe Bach intended as music for the eyes and mind, not music to be played or heard. But most music combines elements of both, and this is certainly the case with most Western art music: a balance between the rhythm of the mind and of the body, between music of revelation and incarnation. So basic is this balance that, as Mellers wrote, it was the

5

subject of 'the first artistically significant opera', Monteverdi's
L'Orfeo (1606).

Mellers made his assertion in *Caliban Reborn*, a book published
in 1967 and, in some ways, with its subtitle 'renewal in twentieth
century music', the inspiration for this book. Mellers believed, and
I believe, that when music is too long out of balance – specifically,
when the balance has shifted too much towards the intellect, the
spiritual, the revelatory – there will be composers who want to
drag it in the opposite direction in order to renew it. It has happened again and again in classical music, but it has also happened
in jazz and in pop. Faced with burgeoning sophistication, musicians have been drawn to what they feel is primitive, 'simple, rude
or rough', drawn to Partch's idea of 'corporeal music' and Mellers's
of 'corporeal rhythm', drawn to the body and to the earth.

Trying to Be Coarse

Thou earth, thou! speak.

Prospero to Caliban, *The Tempest*,
Act 1, Scene 2, William Shakespeare

Nicolai Andreyevich Rimsky-Korsakov (1844–1908) was a suave, rather conservative composer. His music unfolds with well-proportioned inevitability, the melodic lines gracefully shaped, harmony rich and telling; above all, his orchestration is sumptuous. As a colourist, he was, at the start of the twentieth century, in a league of his own. Strauss and Mahler might have been bolder, Debussy more experimental, but no one knew more about the alchemy of the orchestra than Rimsky-Korsakov, and no one combined instrumental timbres with greater refinement.

When I was a student in the 1970s, Rimsky-Korsakov's *Principles of Orchestration* was a set text, and I have it still, its green spine faded to turquoise and cracked through overuse. Musical style had moved on since Rimsky-Korsakov's day, but if a young composer wanted to know how to combine certain instruments to produce a diaphanous shimmer, Rimsky had the answer. And if it was a big sound you were after, with the full orchestra blazing

away, Rimsky and his rarefied ear could advise you in which registers to write your various instruments for maximum effect. There
was nothing this composer did not know about instrumental
nuance, so it comes as a shock to find him writing, on 7 June 1904,
to his colleague Aleksandr Glazunov, 'I am trying to be coarse.'

Rimsky was describing something that had been felt by artists
for centuries, and that continues to be felt. Too much refinement
can obscure the emotional thrust of a work of art; dazzled by its
surface, we fail to attend to the real content of a painting or poem
or piece of music. So the artist goes in search of vulgar means,
partly because they are more direct and partly because rougher
modes of expression are more likely to engage the audience in a
physical manner. This is what Stravinsky meant when he referred
to Schoenberg's *Pierrot lunaire* (1912) as 'the solar plexus as well
as the mind of early twentieth century music'. But the other aspect
of this is the artist's desire to make work that will be recognised
as authentic.

The reason for Rimsky's attempt at vulgarity in 1904 was his
latest opera, *The Legend of the Invisible City of Kitezh and the
Maiden Fevroniya*, a tale of marauding Tartars slaughtering Russians on the banks of the Volga. However much the notion of
coarseness might have gone against his polished grain, Rimsky
obviously believed that this story and these people required some
musical roughing up – not only the Tartars, as he explained to
Glazunov, but the Russians too.

Coarseness is probably in the eye or ear of the beholder, and
anyway it is a moot point how successful Rimsky was in his

project. When the Tartars arrive, they gate-crash the wedding of Prince Vsevolod to the innocent, forest-dwelling Fevroniya, trampling the radiant A major hymn with chromatic harmonies and additive rhythms. The interlude in the middle of Act Three depicts a battle with side drums and cymbal clashes; the drunken Grishka's vision of the Devil finds him repeating terse, jagged fragments of melody, while the orchestra is all downward slithering strings and high trilling winds.

Is this coarse? Not to our modern ears. Indeed, one wonders how coarse Rimsky's contemporaries found it. Perhaps the composer's heart simply wasn't in it. But if Rimsky was not the ideal man for this job, there were plenty of others who were happy to take it on, because what Rimsky was feeling when he wrote to Glazunov was something like peer pressure. 'Trying to be coarse' was a national pastime among Russian artists in the decade and a half before the Revolution, as poets, painters and composers were all drawn to what became known as 'Scythianism'.

The historical Scythians had been a nomadic, horse-riding warrior tribe from somewhere around the central Eurasian steppes, some time between the eighth and fourth centuries BCE. Herodotus mentions them, writing his history in the fifth century BCE, but while he describes their predilection for making drinking vessels of their enemies' skulls, even he is unsure where the Scythians first came from. There is a reference to them in Saint Paul's Epistle to the Colossians, where they are a byword for outlandishness. In a sense, though, the precise geographic origin of the Scythians is of less importance than their foreignness, rootlessness and aggressive nature. Rimsky's Tartars invading the city of Kitezh were latter-day Scythians.

Scythianism in art amounted to an attempt, on the part of musicians, writers and painters, to make their work authentic, raw and real. It was above all nationalistic, because for these artists authenticity meant being Russian and not European. In identifying themselves with the legend of the Scythian tribe, they were underlining their otherness as Russians, their outsider status in relation to the rest of Europe.

Later, Scythianism became a corollary of the revolutionary ideas afoot throughout Europe and especially in Russia itself. Even as Rimsky composed his opera in December 1904, strikes had broken out in the Putilov machinery factory in Saint Petersburg, escalating rather quickly until nearly 100,000 fellow workers were on strike throughout the city. These were the protests that culminated in the Bloody Sunday massacre before the Tsar's Winter Palace on 22 January 1905, when the soldiers of the Imperial Guard fired on an unarmed crowd whose members hoped to present a petition to Nicholas II. Yet while it is tempting to make connections between rough art and revolutionary politics, it would be wrong to think of the artistic movement primarily as revolutionary. Even Leo Tolstoy's donning of peasant garb, although anarcho-Christian in inspiration and non-violent in temperament, might be considered part of this general movement.

More typical, though, was the artistic embrace of the natural world. The overture to *The Invisible City of Kitezh* is designated a 'hymn to the wilderness', and at their first meeting Fevroniya tells

Prince Vsevolod that the forest is her church. The coarseness that Rimsky sought in his music was part of his attempt to portray nature – not only the 'red in tooth and claw' side of nature in the wild, but also, and in particular, the barbarous nature of humankind.

The symbolist poet Aleksandr Blok (1880–1921) is a good example of an artist with Scythian aspirations. Much of Blok's symbolism involved the mention of colours, his work producing a vaguely synaesthetic effect on the reader in that these colours lodge in the mind as one reads, even if one does not know the meanings the poet ascribed to each. In one of Blok's later poems, actually entitled 'The Scythians', he describes the Tartar hoards and their merciless attitude to Europeans (after all, the Tartars have 'nothing to lose'). But it was in his long poem 'The Twelve' that Blok best demonstrated Scythianism in his verse. Written early in 1918, the poem would seem to be an early example of revolutionary art, but in fact it is far more interesting than that would allow. For one thing, Blok's poem is shot through with a heightened mysticism that unexpectedly reveals itself to be pseudo-Christian.

A dozen Bolshevik soldiers tramp through the snowy nighttime streets of Petrograd in the aftermath of the October Revolution. It is in many ways a nightmare scene, told in a jangle of dissonant voices. The colour symbolism here is particularly stark, limited to the black of the night and the white of the snow – especially the latter – with regular splashes of red, most vividly in the form of blood. But in 'The Twelve', Blok's Scythian attitude most clearly reveals itself in the loutish behaviour of the soldiers –

there is a gleeful quality to their vengeful rampage, particularly to their killing of a prostitute called Kat'ka – and in the hyper-colloquial diction employed by the poet, and nicely preserved in Maria Carlson's English translation:

> But where is Kat'ka? 'She's dead, she's dead!
> She's been shot right through the head!'
> Glad now, Kat'ka? 'What, not a peep . . .
> Then lie there, carrion, on the snow!'

The poem is almost an early 'cut-up' of street cries, songs and slogans, with passages from the Orthodox liturgy, its rough-hewn style on the page amplified in contemporary performances by the poet's wife, Liubov Mendeleyeva, who would declaim the poem while lurching about the stage, gesticulating like the ham actor she apparently was.

Contemporary reports of these performances are not kind to Liubov. But then 'The Twelve' itself pleased almost no one. Ramping up the mysticism, Blok hints that the twelve soldiers are a revolutionary version of Christ's apostles. At the end of the poem, indeed, they see ahead of them a vision of a Christ-like figure leading them through the snow. Largely as a result of this, the poem was heavily criticised by actual revolutionaries, who regarded the Christian imagery as anti-revolutionary; Christians, on the other hand, found it blasphemous.

So Scythianism was rough, blunt and fervid, yet also symbolic; looking backwards in order to go forwards, it fashioned modern art out of a peasant past. But its avowed nationalism was about to become international, for in some ways Scythianism reached its apogee in the work of another mystic, Nicholas Roerich (1874–1947), and particularly his collaboration with the composer Igor Stravinsky.

Roerich's early and lasting fascination with archaeology and his later interest in some of the more apocalyptic imagery of Christianity (and other religions) came together in his paintings, both in subject matter and style. Though his images from the early twentieth century are brightly, even garishly, coloured, they are far from modernist in nature, mostly depicting scenes from Russian peasant life. Still, so far, so Scythian. But his work as a designer for Sergei Diaghilev's Ballets Russes would bring things to a head.

In Diaghilev's company, designers were hugely important, virtually auteurs, and this was the role Roerich played in the Ballets Russes' most famous creation, *The Rite of Spring* (1913). Its composer, Stravinsky, claimed that the image of a virgin's sacrificial dance had come to him in a dream, and this may well have been true (though Stravinsky was an inveterate self-mythologiser). What is beyond doubt is that the detailed scenario of *The Rite* was down to Roerich, and since the score of *The Rite* is ballet music in the strictest sense – music designed to tell a story – not only its mood of studied barbarism but also its very structure came from Roerich's imagination at least as much as from Stravinsky's.

There are, of course, other instances of Scythianism in art. Among musical works, Sergei Prokofiev's *Scythian Suite* (1915) is the most obvious example, its insistently brutal orchestral palette conceived for a Scythian ballet, *Ala and Lolly*, commissioned by Diaghilev for the Ballets Russes, then cancelled even before the score was completed (the suite was an act of salvage on its composer's part). But throughout the whole of Europe and further afield, the first decades of the twentieth century – the years before, during and after the Great War – produced numerous works that dealt in barbarism of one sort or another, works that set out to be brutal or basic, rude or rough and, above all, 'progressive'. Edgard Varèse's massive orchestral pieces *Amériques* (1918–21) and *Arcana* (1925) can seem almost like extensions of the music of *The Rite of Spring*, but works as different as Arnold Schoenberg's one-act musical dramas *Erwartung* (1909) and *Die glückliche Hand* (1913), Alban Berg's first opera *Wozzeck* (1914–22), Leoš Janáček's orchestral suite *Taras Bulba* (1915–18) and his opera *From the House of the Dead* (1927), and Béla Bartók's ballet *The Miraculous Mandarin* (1918–24) all deal in extreme sounds and subject matter.

These same years witnessed similar trends in theatre, literature and the visual arts. From the fat, farting, murderous anti-hero of Alfred Jarry's play *Ubu Roi* (as early as 1896) to the syntax-defying experiments in James Joyce's *Ulysses* (1914–21) and *The Cantos* of Ezra Pound (begun in 1915) to the garish colours and thick paint of the Fauves (or 'wild beasts') and the Cubists, the often brutal energy on stage, page and canvas went hand-in-glove with new forms and modes of expression. Trying to be coarse in one way or another was the unholy grail of the early modernists.

* * *

But if the early twentieth century offered one of the most consist-ent and sustained examples of musical primitivism, it was really nothing new. Here is the composer Christoph Willibald Gluck in 1774 dedicating the score of *Orphée et Euridice* (the new French version of his opera *Orfeo ed Euridice*) to his former pupil, Marie Antoinette: 'The style that I attempt to introduce seems to me to restore to art its primitive dignity, and music will no longer be restricted to those cold conventional beauties to which authors were formerly forced to confine themselves.'

That phrase 'primitive dignity' ('dignité primitive') is interest-ing. Gluck implies that he has pared back the style of his music to something basic, something true. If it was not so much coarse-ness that he was after, it was certainly simplicity and directness. And freshness, as well. Gluck argued that opera had become clut-tered by affectation; he wanted to make it more realistic – or as realistic as possible, given the on-stage circumstances of people singing to each other on a trip to the underworld. He also wanted to move the drama along musically, to make the music serve human characters with real emotions and not 'cold conventional beauties' ('froides beautés de convention'). In this regard, he was harking back to Monteverdi and *L'Orfeo* 150 years earlier. These things go in cycles.

Ultimately, the desire to be more real and more human lies behind most attempts to be primitive in music, whether it involves seeking coarseness, confronting and sometimes celebrating bru-tality, or simplifying the means of expression either by employing the most basic musical building blocks or by composing in a more basic manner. It nearly always implies some sort of looking back, an intention to return to a musical sound or structure (real or imagined, it hardly matters) that is closer to our 'ordinary' human experience, often more connected to the human body, earthier. And it nearly always aims at or results in something new, music that is bolder, fresher or more vigorous.

One might argue that the common Renaissance conceit of quoting popular songs in settings of the Mass was an early attempt to admit the influence of the outside world to a complex polyphonic structure and indeed to the church: secular 'roughness' at the service of the spiritual. There were various approaches, including parody or imitation Masses which quoted short sections from other pieces – often secular motets – as well as cyclic Masses in which four- or five-part polyphony was built on the long, slow notes of a *cantus firmus* derived from another source; Dufay's *Missa L'homme armé* is an early example. In 1562 the Council of Trent, perhaps sensing a whiff of reformation about the practice, insisted that the use of secular material in liturgical contexts be abandoned, though it continued even after the edict. Occasionally the songs employed were *extremely* secular. As late as 1581, the great Flemish master Orlande de Lassus wrote his *Missa Entre vous filles* for five voices, based on a particularly scurrilous song by Clemens non Papa in praise of the breasts and vaginas – *tétins* and *connins* – of fifteen-year-old girls.

Smut aside, it has been composers' continual attraction to the sound of the unschooled, the demotic, the 'other' in music that has most characterised their desire to be earthy. This began in earnest during the baroque, though recognising such earthiness today often requires a leap of imagination. When, for example, we listen to the music of Jean-Philippe Rameau (1683–1764), it is hard to credit the accusations of barbarism levelled at him by supporters of his rival Lully. One of these critics was the dramatist Jean-Baptiste Rousseau. Writing of Rameau's opera *Dardanus*, he ordered the composer to flee, make way for Lully and cease 'grating the ears of good people'. It sounds horrific. But the music doesn't. Even a piece called 'Les sauvages' from Rameau's opera-ballet *Les Indes galantes* (1735) is unlikely to grate the most sensitive of modern ears. On the contrary, these 'savages' are given a perky little rondo, and when we read that their music was inspired by the sight of native Americans dancing at a Parisian theatre, Rameau's music seems more like transcontinental kitsch than something that is genuinely rough or rude. Perhaps you had to be present to have your ears grated.

By comparison, Haydn's use of modal melodic lines above drones still delivers a sonic punch. Joseph Haydn (1732–1809) might have spent most of his working life holed up in the palace at Eszterháza, some sixty kilometres from Vienna, but it is clear from his music that he got out a lot and was greatly impressed by the sound of hurdy-gurdies and bagpipes in the surrounding countryside. In Haydn's symphonies and string quartets, particularly those of his later years, there are numerous moments that testify to this composer's fascination with the music of the Austro-Hungarian *volk*.

Typically, they occur in the trio section of a minuet (the third movement of Symphony No 88 contains an example that, in the right hands, can still seem shocking) or in the finale. In the last movement of Haydn's String Quartet Op 74, No 1, for example, the good spirits and easy diatonicism that characterise most of the music keep getting derailed when the viola and cello become stuck on a C/G drone, while the violins, in octaves, present a chromatic tune with some Lydian-mode leanings suggestive of bagpipes. Symphony No 82 is nicknamed 'The Bear' for its bear-dance finale, underpinned by an insistent, pulsing C, sometimes preceded by a scoop up from the note below it – the effect one hears when a set of bagpipes is inflated. But the most famous example of a drone in a Haydn finale comes in his last symphony, No 104 in D, which is generally known as the 'London' symphony, though its German nickname is 'Sinfonie mit dem Dudelsack' (symphony with bag-pipes), a reference to the octave Ds that run as a drone through the first bars.

Composers had been using folk tunes in their work for centu-ries before Haydn, but like many of his baroque predecessors, Haydn was particularly interested in dramatic effect: he was drawn to folk music not only for its melodic distinction, but also for the sound it made. In this regard he is a direct predecessor of Stravin-sky and Bartók. But in Haydn's wide embrace of the world beyond his work desk, it sometimes seems a small step from his sympho-nies to those of Mahler or Charles Ives, where the concert hall will suddenly be invaded by a dance band or a marching band – or, in Ives's case, six marching bands.

With composers such as Stravinsky and Bartók, the rough and sometimes aggressive sound of peasant music came to dominate whole pieces. In Stravinsky's ballet *Les noces* ('The Wedding', 1914–23), not only was the work full of folk songs and folk-song fragments, sung and shouted by the soloists and the chorus of wedding guests, but the composer also invented a new instrumental combination to project the intense rhythmic dynamism of the music, pitching his singers into a modernist sound world of bright colours and harsh dissonances, free from sentimentality. After much experimentation – jettisoning first an enormous, 150-piece orchestra in favour of a range of on-stage ensembles that would include a cimbalom (the Hungarian hammered dulcimer), a harpsichord and a piano, then trying a mechanical player-piano with harmonium, percussion and *two* cimbaloms – Stravinsky finally settled on the unlikely combination of four pianos and a truckload of percussion instruments, requiring six performers. The resulting piece, despite the pale imitations of Carl Orff, remains thrillingly unique.

One of the few pieces that come close to it is *Three Village Scenes* (1926) by Bartók. It is a version of the last three of five songs for soprano and piano (also called *Village Scenes*) and a tribute of sorts to *Les noces*. A women's chorus sings genuine Slovakian songs – the first actually about a wedding – while a mixed ensemble, piano and snare drum to the fore, make clangorous, dissonant interjections. Bartók was an enthusiastic and inveterate collector of folk music ('I have travelled on awful roads and in terrible carriages,' he wrote on one expedition in 1914), but he never failed to identify those aspects of traditional music that could bring something real, urgent and *new* to his compositions. Both *Les noces* and *Three Village Scenes* – and many more pieces by those composers – blend ancient and modern, poet and peasant, body and soul. But it is also important to remember that these scores were composed for the ballet theatre and concert hall, and that to appreciate their significance we must view them through a lens of 'high art'. Like Haydn before them, Stravinsky and Bartók were dragging not only demotic tunes but also demotic noise into these establishments, in the process roughing up the bourgeois sensitivities of many in the audience.

The raw sound of Janáček's *Sinfonietta* (1926) is apparent at once, courtesy of the extra brass players – including nine trumpets – the composer called for. They were not just any trumpet players: Janáček had been impressed by the sonority of a military band and wanted to emulate it in the fanfares that open and close this work, his last for orchestra. Ideally, this was to be achieved by importing actual military brass players, but should they prove thin on the ground, the composer advised, regular players would suffice, so long as they played like the trumpeters of a military band – as brashly as possible. It was the sound he was after.

Janáček's inspiration, cultural and political, was Czech national identity – his *Sinfonietta* is dedicated to the 'Czechoslovakian Armed Forces' – and it may be readily heard in most of his mature music, especially the melodic lines. Typically, they have a torn-off quality, the melodic cells stitched together to form longer patterns, though with a good deal of fragmentation and repetition. These themes reflect not only the folk music of the composer's Moravian birthplace but also Czech speech patterns. Like Musorgsky before him in his operas and song cycles, Janáček reasoned that if folk song was an extension of native speech and its rhythms, he could draw on speech itself for his own musical purposes. It was naturalistic and also, in Janáček's case, nationalistic.

There was, doubtless, also an element of patriotism in Bartók's use of folk music, but more important to the Hungarian was the notion that his research might be the key to finding an antidote to Romantic excess. In 1931 he wrote that 'peasant music' has an 'amazing' expressive power, yet 'is devoid of all sentimentality and superfluous ornaments. It is simple, sometimes primitive, but never silly. It is the ideal starting point for a musical renaissance, and a composer in search of new ways cannot be led by a better master.' He goes on to recommend that composers who want to avail themselves of this 'starting point' had better study the music thoroughly in order to avoid the pitfalls of dilettantism; they must assimilate the folk idiom so that it is inseparable from their own style.

No one could argue that Australian-born Percy Grainger (1882–1961) failed in this last regard. Not only did he study and assimilate the music, he identified with it every bit as much as Bartók. Like Bartók, Grainger viewed folk music as a way forward for his own work and for composed music in general. The big difference between Grainger and Bartók was in their attitudes to 'Romantic excess'. Grainger – always in search of harmonic emotion and never one to be hidebound by good taste – happily embraced excess in many areas of his life. His folk-song settings inhabited a harmonic world not far removed from that of the Victorian parlour song, but as Grainger's songs progressed, they typically accrued extra chromaticism, risking, embracing and finally transcending sentimentality.

Where Bartók had drawn on the sound of folk music, Grainger had attempted to reveal its deep humanity. For many music lovers, he had gone too far and strayed into kitsch.

When concert-hall composers draw on music from outside their own area – from folk music, from jazz or rock, from the music of other cultures – kitsch is always the danger. The Canadian composer Colin McPhee (1900–64) is a good example. He is rightly famous as the first Western composer to make a serious and systematic study of the music of Bali. In the early 1940s he shared both a house and his ethno-musicological findings with Benjamin Britten, the two composers making a recording of McPhee's two-piano arrangements, entitled *Balinese Ceremonial Music*. But McPhee's own music, which was inspired by the music of Bali, is less successful. His best-known piece, *Tabuh-Tabuhan* (1936), was for an orchestra with a small 'nuclear gamelan' at its heart, consisting of two pianos, a couple of tuned gongs and a range of keyboard percussion. When this group plays, the music has a refreshing sparkle about it, but as soon as the rest of the orchestra – the 'Western' part – enters, we find ourselves in the realm of bad film music. Put simply, it's kitsch.

Britten, on the other hand, absorbed what he learnt from McPhee, the influence of gamelan surfacing almost at once in the 'Sunday Morning' sea interlude in *Peter Grimes* (1945). No Suffolk church bells ever rang out with the patterns that Britten gave them here, but equally the music sounds nothing like gamelan; indeed, most listeners would probably fail to notice that gamelan is behind it. Britten's interlude just sounds bright and strong and new. And perhaps it is the ability of a great composer to find in unfamiliar music something that seems familiar, and to bring that influence quickly and easily into their own work – to make it their own – that distinguishes genuine and important art from art that is at best decorative, and at worst cliché or kitsch. It is what distinguishes the late music of the Hungarian György Ligeti (1923–2006), deeply influenced by the rhythmic devices found in the music of sub-Saharan Africa, from, say, David Fanshawe's *African Sanctus* (1972).

True kitsch is never knowing. Its creator must at least be aiming to be serious, and McPhee and Fanshawe undoubtedly were. So was John Antill when he composed his ballet *Corroboree* (1946). He had witnessed Aboriginal corroborees in Sydney as a boy, and was perfectly genuine in his wish to capture and convey their spirit in his ballet score. Unlike McPhee, Antill did not attempt to use Aboriginal music in his work – though there is the sound of clap sticks and, more contentiously, a bullroarer – so that does not account for the kitsch elements in his score. On the contrary, among a certain amount of originality in *Corroboree*, it is those passages that emulate *The Rite of Spring* that are hardest to take seriously, second-hand Stravinsky tending towards kitsch in the scores of many a mid-twentieth-century composer; one thinks, again, of Orff, whose *Carmina Burana* (1936) is kitsch from start to finish. Antill later claimed that when he composed *Corroboree*, he had not yet heard *The Rite of Spring*. This does seem unlikely, given that he had already spent a decade in the music department of the Australian Broadcasting Commission (as it then was). But if he hadn't heard *The Rite*, he had surely heard the music of composers who had been influenced by it, which would make those derivative pages of *Corroboree* third-hand Stravinsky.

* * *

When Western composers have drawn inspiration from music that traditionally remains outside the concert hall, they have usually done so in order to free their music from convention, stripping away bad habits and tired thinking in pursuit of new energy and ideas. But the appropriation of popular culture is only one aspect of this. The impulse to rediscover something primitive in art has been recurrent through history, and as often as not this has come down to artists relying on their own instincts, their own emotions and their own experience, aligning the real world with the interior world of the imagination.

When, for example, Monteverdi and his contemporaries wrote the first operas at the start of the seventeenth century, they attempted to bring something of the quality of heightened speech to their vocal lines. This representative style (*stile rappresentativo*) came from a dramatic imperative – that same imperative that would inform Gluck's vision of opera in the eighteenth century: if audiences were to be engaged by the story, they had to be able to understand and believe the words, so the more speech-like, the better. Set beside a dense slab of sixteenth-century polyphony, this new style still makes a bold contrast, one that is not only closer to reality, but also far simpler. Here is another common feature of the urge to return to something primitive: that music should be less complex.

One can hear this in the harmonic structure of the early Classical style – bold, clean diatonicism, in contrast to the rich chromaticism of the high baroque. It is there in the sleek lines of 1920s neo-classicism, after the large-scale explosions of early modernism. The simple pentatonic repetitions of early minimalism offer another rather obvious example, following on from the harsh complexities – harmonic, rhythmic and textural – of the post–World War II avant-garde.

Evidently, the primitive urge in one form or another is particularly strong at certain moments in history, and there will always be composers who, of their own volition, want to make their music more energised or coarse. Early twentieth-century Russia was one such historical moment, early nineteenth-century Vienna another, and Ludwig van Beethoven was one of those composers.

It hardly needs to be pointed out that Beethoven was capable of great refinement in his music, of great complexity and great lyricism. These were all aspects of his musical range – perhaps the greatest range of any artist this side of Shakespeare. But equally, Beethoven could be blunt, terse, simple, raw, rough and even violent, and it had nothing to do with folk music. There are, in fact, a few, mostly rather polite, folk-song settings by Beethoven, but they seem tangential to his music, even incongruous in that great, masterpiece-studded body of work. This was not a composer who required vernacular music to help him find his own vigour. And while it is certainly possible to point to the times in which Beethoven lived and to associate the belligerence in some of his music with Enlightenment philosophy, revolutionary politics and the first flowering of Romanticism, the truth is that Beethoven himself was partly responsible for those times.

To take only famous examples, one could cite the composer's remarkable liberation of rhythm as a unifying element in music (throughout his Symphony No 5 in C minor) and occasionally as thematic material (the second movement of the String Quartet in F, Op 59, No 1). In the first movement of Symphony No 6 in F (*Pastoral*), the development section is utterly without precedent in basing itself on a fragment from the middle of the first theme, then gently repeating it for long stretches – like some sort of minimalist trance music – varying the pitches and harmony, but not the rhythm.

Another aspect of Beethoven's attraction to more primitive modes of expression is in the sound of his music, and particularly in his willingness to be ugly when that is what the musical material or its development requires. One thinks first of the cacophonous outburst at the start of the finale of the ninth symphony, that angry clearing away of everything that had gone before, an act of musical rebellion – Beethoven's own music, as it were, rising up against itself. Beethoven proceeds to rake through the debris of the first three movements, briefly quoting from each in turn, before introducing the famous 'Ode to Joy' theme, at the end of which the original outburst returns, more violent than before. Violent really is the word, because the gesture wipes out what we have just heard, and into the empty space steps something no less startling in a symphony: a human voice singing the poet Schiller's words: 'O Freunde, nicht diese Töne!' – 'Oh friends, not these sounds!'

One thinks, also, of the still astonishing *Grosse Fuge*, Op 133, the 'great fugue' that Beethoven originally proposed for the finale of his late String Quartet in B flat, Op 130. Perhaps the single most astonishing thing about this fifteen-minute exercise in high drama is its fusion of a complex form and often complex contrapuntal texture with a level of raw energy never before approached by a string quartet. It is the energy in particular that sticks in the mind, and also the sense of struggle. This is not simply music 'about' struggle – the music *is* the struggle. Harrison Birtwistle (born 1934) once said of his own music that, had he been a sculptor, you would be able to see the chisel marks in his work, and here Beethoven is showing his chisel marks. At the outset of the *Grosse Fuge*, in the so-called 'Overtura', Beethoven lays out his materials, his themes and counter-themes – indeed, 'lays out' is too polite a term, as he throws them down before us – and for the remainder of the piece we listen as he works furiously to bring it all together: his frustration is in the music, and so is his anger. In the finale of the ninth symphony, we heard fragments of music that had gone before, but here we're presented with fragments of music that is still to come, still to be put together like some IKEA fugue that will enrage the composer as he assembles it.

The first attempt, a double fugue, is in fact perfectly achieved, and the counterpoint would surely have pleased Bach. But Bach would have been amazed and possibly affronted by the aggression of the music, for this is a fugue that shouts at us. It is marked *forte*, and it remains that way to the end, except for those moments when

Beethoven increases the dynamic from *f* to *ff*. It wasn't only fugues that Beethoven was building in his late music, it was also German Romanticism, because all this sound and fury signified a very great deal: the self-conscious artist, the artist as humanist, the artist as hero of the Enlightenment. For the next century – arguably for the next two – the composers who followed Beethoven would have to deal with his example. Out of Beethoven's return to basic materials came another new cycle of musical growth.

* * *

In the short history of rock music, similar cyclical developments can be discerned, only the wheel has turned rather faster. From early rock and roll in the mid-1950s – guitar, bass and drums playing three chords for two minutes – it was barely a decade before the Beatles' *Revolver* (1966) and *Sgt Pepper's Lonely Heart's Club Band* (1967), with their string quartets, sitars and tape collages, the Beach Boys' *Pet Sounds* (1966) and Pink Floyd's *The Piper at the Gates of Dawn* (1967). At the end of the 1960s, bands such as Creedence Clearwater Revival still continued to play straight-ahead rock (albeit at greater length than two minutes), but once again the musical style escalated, so that by the mid-1970s, bands such as Yes, King Crimson, and Emerson, Lake & Palmer were scarcely suited to the term 'rock band' at all. Then there was punk, first in New York with the Ramones and then in England, and it was back to three chords, if you were lucky. But out of punk, and indeed made by punk, came sophisticated songwriters of the likes of David Byrne and Elvis Costello. And then, suddenly, along came Violent

Femmes, a Milwaukee band dedicated, in the words of their bass-ist, Brian Ritchie, to 'trying to bring punk back to a Woody Guthrie/Robert Johnson/Buddy Bolden vibe by playing acoustic instruments on the street'. All that, in just twenty-five years.

With each reversion to something more basic came a new ele-ment of rebellion. Today this is hard to credit, but from the first chorus of 'Rock Around the Clock' rock and roll had always been associated with transgression. It was meant to be dangerous, pro-vocative, loud and beyond the comprehension and control of par-ents; if it wasn't these things, then it wasn't rock and roll. And it was sexual. Again, we may look at grainy black-and-white footage of Elvis Presley and marvel at the hysterical response of both his fans and their parents to those swivelling hips, but when Frank Sinatra listened to Elvis in 1957, he heard songs that were 'sly, lewd – in plain fact, dirty'.

Almost as outrageous as Elvis's hips was Jerry Lee Lewis's long hair – which, by the standards of even ten years later, was not very long at all. The growl in Buddy Holly's voice as he sang, 'Rrrrave on,' was clearly at odds with the trademark innocence of the 'Uh-weh-uh-heh-uh-ell' that had began that song ('Rave On', 1958). And could it really be that Little Richard was wearing makeup? These sounds and signs were all a long way from Perry Como crooning 'Magic Moments', which many white, middle-class parents would have preferred their children to be spending their pocket money on. But there was something more to these early rockers that worried the white middle classes: some of these new singers were black, but even those who weren't *sounded* black.

For the predominantly white record-buying, radio-listening, TV-watching public in the mostly segregated United States of the 1950s, sexuality and black skin was a volatile mix. This was something Chuck Berry understood well as he duck-walked across the stage, his guitar neck bobbing up and down priapically. Berry's ability to provoke alarm was enhanced by the colour of his skin, and in front of his large white audience he played on it, as had many blues and jazz musicians before him, with songs such as 'Brown-eyed Handsome Man' (1956), in which he flaunted his sexuality in a specifically racial way. Berry was a master lyricist, and his songs made much use of wordplay and irony. In 'Brown-eyed Handsome Man', it is not only the man's eyes that are brown but also his skin, while the succession of women who take pity on our hero are, by heavy implication, white.

> The judge's wife called up the district attorney,
> Said, 'You free that brown-eyed man!'

Berry, who had himself had been in gaol, but whose stage manner was always rather debonair (like his lyrics), was making fun of the white suspicion of the stereotypical promiscuous black man.

> Back ever since the world began
> There's been a whole lot of good women shed a tear
> For a brown-eyed handsome man

But if Berry was mocking the fear of miscegenation, a year earlier Muddy Waters was stoking it with the swaggering braggadocio of 'Mannish Boy' (1955). There is very little sophistication here, just raw energy and a rough voice. Muddy Waters half-sings, half-hollers this song, above an endlessly repeating guitar riff (a single chord – in effect, a drone), promising all the women 'out there in line' that he will be able to satisfy them 'in five minutes' time'. In the chorus, he reiterates, 'I'm a man'; that is, a man and *not* a 'boy'. This is a song not only of macho boasting but also of racial pride, its power reinforced by its pared-back musical delivery.

The electric blues of Chicago in the 1950s and early 1960s, typified by 'Mannish Boy', was one of those moments in musical history when 'simple, rude or rough' sounds bring renewal, when urgency replaces refinement and clears a path for a fresh direction. In the industrialised north of the United States, the twelve- and sixteen-bar blues templates was powered by electricity, giving them an often searing effect, not only because of the increased volume but also because the electric guitar and amplified harmonica could scream and wail and create considerably more raw energy than their acoustic counterparts. The music of Muddy Waters and Willie Dixon, Howlin' Wolf and Sonny Boy Williamson II, Little Walter and Etta James led, in short order, to rhythm and blues bands in the early 1960s, particularly in the United Kingdom. The Rolling Stones, the Animals, Them (featuring Van Morrison) and the Yardbirds (featuring Jimmy Page and Eric Clapton and, later, Jeff Beck) all sang songs associated with the aforementioned Chicago blues performers, the rawness preserved in music that contrasted sharply with the more saccharine end of British pop.

But already the musical style was beginning to inflate. With Cream and Led Zeppelin, Clapton and Page took this music to a different level, one of greater virtuosity and more extended and sophisticated structures. Jimi Hendrix, an American based in the United Kingdom, topped them both in these departments. Simultaneously, heavy metal bands on both sides of the Atlantic – such as Deep Purple and Black Sabbath – though less sophisticated musically, were yet more ambitious in the scale of their work. Although still using the harmonic templates and melodic shapes of the blues, bands as different as Kiss and AC/DC in the 1970s and 1980s were bigger in just about every other sense: they played longer and louder and in vast stadiums. So powerful had the music become that, faced with the arrival of punk rock, rather than collapsing under the weight of their own pretensions, new metal bands emerged with punk fully absorbed as an influence and a sound that was rawer and still more aggressive. This is precisely why Violent Femmes wanted to reclaim punk.

* * *

As T.S. Eliot pointed out, 'to make an end is to make a beginning', and in all the arts, the return to something more primitive has nearly always been the seed of a new development. Often, out of the 'simple, rude or rough', there emerges art of greater refinement and sophistication, which in turn leads to new, complex and ambitious structures and strategems. Two parallel examples of this lie in the work of the painter Wassily Kandinsky (1866–1944) and the composer Arnold Schoenberg (1874–1951).

Kandinsky was a contemporary and compatriot of Nicholas Roerich and, in the first decade of the twentieth century, much of their art was almost interchangeable. Kandinsky's subject matter was perhaps less inclined to mysticism, but the colours, textures and shapes of their work – especially landscapes and villages – drew on Russian folk art and a somewhat idealised version of peasant life. For Kandinsky, this did not last. Although he might have shared Roerich's aesthetics, Kandinsky, more Fauve than Scythian, was at heart a cosmopolitan fellow.

By 1908 and 1909, around the time Schoenberg and his pupils, Alban Berg and Anton Webern, were composing their first atonal pieces – which were really anyone's first atonal pieces – Kandinsky's colours had grown more lurid and his shapes less inclined to resemble a farmhouse or a tree. In music, Kandinsky recognised a level of abstraction to which he now aspired in his painting, but he also hoped to go further, freeing colour from form. In Schoenberg's new pieces, he heard an example of how that might be done, the composer having untethered musical pitch from its centuries-old hierarchy of key relationships: pitches were now permitted to be themselves, and timbre – or tone *colour* – often played as important a role as pitch in the structure of a line or block of sound. After attending a concert of Schoenberg's music in early 1911, Kandinsky produced his abstract painting 'Impression III (Concert)'. He also wrote the composer a letter, initiating a long correspondence between the two men.

Schoenberg, who at this point in his career was a painter as well as a composer, found in Kandinsky both a fan and a kindred spirit. But what these two artists were achieving with colour and pitch was not merely abstract and dissonant, for Schoenberg's stage works of the period were also vivid examples of expressionism, in which the unconscious mind and the world of dreams and nightmares was now the stuff of art. That this should be taking place in Sigmund Freud's Vienna was hardly a matter of coincidence. In giving people access to their unconscious states and permission to explore them, Freud was opening up fertile ground for artists, particularly those with an interest in the primitive. 'Art belongs to the *unconscious!*' Schoenberg wrote to Kandinsky. You could argue that the human unconscious was the ultimate primitive state.

Schoenberg's *Erwartung* ('Expectation') is a monodrama for soprano and large orchestra with a relatively simple, dream-like scenario. A woman stumbles through a moonlit forest in a state of agitation. She is searching for her lover, and at length discovers his bloodied corpse. Maybe she has killed him herself. Maybe it is all a bad dream. The music, intensely expressive and always plunging forwards, bears the listener on as though through a nightmare; there are even moments in which the music emulates that feeling of running but going nowhere.

From the point of view of its dramatic content, the composer's next stage work, *Die glückliche Hand*, was more extreme. The title translates as 'The Fortunate Hand' or, more idiomatically, 'The Knack', and the piece concerns a man, indeed an artist, who in the first scene we discover trapped face-down beneath 'a cat-like, fantastic animal (hyena with enormous, bat-like wings) that seems to have sunk its teeth into his neck'. A chorus of six female and six male voices, representing something like a cross between the artist's muse and his unconscious, taunt and goad him, telling him that he may struggle all he likes but will never win. The artist then dreams of two silent figures – a woman and a gentleman ('Ein Herr'). The woman distracts the artist from his work and encourages him to abandon his high ideals; she behaves seductively towards him, but then runs off with the gentleman. In the final scene, the vampire-like creature is back, once more pinning the artist down and biting into his neck as the muse/unconscious calls the man 'Du Armer!' – 'You pathetic fool!'

You do not need to know very much about psychoanalysis to see that these pieces contain some textbook stuff. The libretto of *Erwartung* was written by Marie Pappenheim, a former pupil of Freud's and sister of the famous 'Anna O', whom Freud and Josef Breuer had written about in *Studies on Hysteria* (1895). However, the imagery in *Die glückliche Hand* of the silent female as siren, succubus and harpy came not from Freud – at least not directly – but from Otto Weininger's book *Sex and Character*. Weininger published his treatise-*cum*-diatribe in 1903 at the age of twenty-three. This was also the year of his suicide, the young writer shooting himself in the head in a rented room in the house where his hero Beethoven had died. Among many equally contentious theories, Weininger posited men as the innocent victims of libidinous female sexuality. The playwright August Strindberg considered him a genius, and so, for a time, did Schoenberg.

But Schoenberg's music and Kandinsky's paintings were far more than the unfettered outpourings of their unconscious minds (inspired, in the case of *Die glückliche Hand*, by a crazy misogynist). Their works and some of their pronouncements in the years leading to the outbreak of World War I might have made them seem like revolutionaries, but in fact they had a rather traditional outlook, and both were also theorists. In the year that their friendship began, each published his first book. Kandinsky's *On the Spiritual in Art* and Schoenberg's *Harmonielehre* demonstrated that their authors were more concerned with order than their art might have suggested. In Schoenberg's case, having plumbed the murkier depths of the human mind in *Erwartung* and *Die glückliche Hand*, and having done so with a harmonic palette that was effectively anarchic – since the system of keys had been swept away, to be replaced only by relativity of pitch – a new order was urgently needed.

In an essay written around 1930, Schoenberg looked back at *Erwartung* and *Die glückliche Hand* to explain what, for him, had been the real interest in composing these works. It had nothing to do with Freud or Weininger, dreams or the unconscious, sex or death: it was all about form. Schoenberg wrote that in *Erwartung* his intention had been 'to represent in *slow motion* everything that occurs during a single second of maximum spiritual excitement, stretching it out to half an hour, whereas in *Die glückliche Hand* a major drama is compressed into about 20 minutes, as if photographed with a time exposure'. A century on, when the subject matter of these pieces can seem – to be blunt – a bit silly, one can only agree with Schoenberg.

36

By the time Schoenberg wrote his essay, his music had changed in one very important respect. Now it had rules, and quite strict ones at that. In 1913, composing his six tiny Bagatelles for string quartet, Schoenberg's pupil Webern had already found that he was writing out the twelve possible chromatic pitches and crossing each one off as he used it. He said that he came to feel that when he had used each pitch once, the piece was over. This, of course, goes some way to explaining the extreme brevity of the music – taken together, the six little pieces last just over three minutes – but it also demonstrates, in a very practical manner, how twelve-tone music came into being. It would be another decade before the concept was codified and Schoenberg could proclaim the first serial piece, but here was the system in embryo.

The primitive impulse that had been evident in Schoenberg's music and Kandinsky's painting before the Great War cleared a path for greater refinement and stricter control. After 1923, Schoenberg's music was almost exclusively serial, and so was that of his pupils. The structures they used were often rather tight and formal, adaptations of old, ready-made forms such as baroque dances, Classical sonata form (or a version of it) and canons. Similarly, the dynamism of Kandinsky's early abstracts was tamed, his structures became more balanced, his shapes gained harder edges, and the power of his colours was harnessed, rather than leaping from the canvas.

Webern's music in particular took on a beautiful rigour, its formal surface a meshing of geometrically elegant phrases, intervals and single, isolated notes, often in canonic form. Webern was a dedicated amateur botanist and extremely interested in crystal-lography. Perhaps knowing this led some early critics and perform-ers to represent his music as cool and austere. But you only have to read Webern's letters to Berg and Schoenberg, describing, often in fervent language, his study of Alpine flora, to realise that he felt considerable passion for the natural world and wanted his music to reflect this. Even so, from a structural point of view, his pieces do display an element of control that can be compared with his scientific studies, and the fact that this interest was in small forms – wildflowers and so forth – also seems appropriate. Though his pieces of the 1920s, '30s and '40s were never again as brief as those Bagatelles, they remained very much miniatures. His longest work, which was also his last, was Cantata No 2, settings of texts by the naturalist–poet Hildegard Jone. The piece lasts just a quarter of an hour, and even then it comprises six movements. Moreover, a musical style that, before World War I, had exploded from the creative unconscious in mysterious whispers and jagged dis-sonances, by the time of World War II had become the height of refinement, 'stripped', as Robert Craft wrote, 'of all ornament'.

After 1945, the year of Webern's death, some young compos-ers in Europe came to regard his music as a way forward. There was, after all, something ascetic about it, and it is not hard to see why it might have seemed like a clean slate – Pierre Boulez, one of those young composers, spoke of a 'zero hour'. But in music, extreme refinement always leads to its polar opposite. The cycle always plays out. Boulez himself, in his second piano sonata (1948), written when he was just twenty-three, took Webern's example in a radical new direction, composing a piece that was more than three times longer than the longest piece by his Viennese forebear, that required the same sort of virtuosity needed to play the music of Liszt, that had the emotional intensity of a modern *Hammerklavier* sonata, and that included instructions to the player, at one point, to 'pulverise the sound'. It was grander and more ambitious than anything Webern had attempted, even if the basic model was still much in evidence. Other composers completed the cycle more persuasively, responding to Webern's example with music that was starker and once more primitive.

The Russian Galina Ustvolskaya (1919–2006) insisted that her own music was a new beginning, that she had created her own 'zero hour', but her work had quite a bit in common with that of Webern. First, there was a kind of purity that, in Ustvolskaya's case, approached fanaticism. For example, she wanted her music performed in churches, not concert halls, and only by men. Such extreme attitudes are amply reflected in the sound and nature of her music, in which Webern's small cells and individual notes are either barely audible or hammered home: there were no ornaments here either. In Ustvolskaya's Piano Sonata No 6 (1988), for example, there are passages in which the performer must produce tone clusters at a regular tempo and the unrelentingly loud dynamic of *ffff*. As in Webern's music, the single note or sound is given a rare prominence, often a separate identity, but the violent brutality of execution here had no precedent in Webern or even Boulez. It is hard to sit through a performance of this piece without fearing for the wellbeing of the piano. Sometimes it is just hard to sit through.

There appears to have been a spiritual imperative to Ustvolskaya's music. It might not have had much to do with the more comforting spirituality found in the music of her contemporary Arvo Pärt, but there is something ineffable about her work. However, for the Greek composer Iannis Xenakis (1922–2001), inspiration was more down-to-earth. In Olivier Messiaen's composition class in Paris during the early 1950s, he had met other young modernists, such as Karlheinz Stockhausen and Jean Barraqué. The music of Schoenberg, Berg and Webern was just becoming known in the French capital in the years after World War II. Xenakis embraced its atonality, but had little use for its serial methods, still less its Viennese accent. Where Webern's music consisted of pinpricks of sound – the plinks and plonks of popular dismissal, and a texture much emulated in those years, not least by Messiaen in his piano piece 'Modes de valeurs et d'intensités' and by Stockhausen in *Kreuzspiel* – Xenakis, from the start, created great sheets and slabs of sound. In terms of technique, the aggressive attacks on the piano in Ustvolskaya's sixth sonata find plenty of parallels in the music of Xenakis (who was just as happy to write a quadruple forte dynamic indication), and so does the quality of relentlessness. But it is the sheets and slabs that make the most impact.

Great teacher that he was, Messiaen spotted that Xenakis was no good at conventional harmony, and understood that this was simply an aspect of the young man's very specific talents. Messiaen encouraged Xenakis to take a more architectural approach to his music, and this eventually led him to design works graphically before fleshing them out in sound. It helped that the Greek composer's other passion was for architecture itself, and that his other Parisian mentor was Le Corbusier, in whose studio he worked and with whom he would collaborate on the design of the famous Dominican priory of Sainte Marie de la Tourette near Lyon, in the south of France.

Metastaseis (1953–54) is a typically bold example of Xenakis's early music, an orchestral work in which each player has an individual line – there are, for example, forty-six separate string parts. The fact that this music was mapped out at an architect's drawing board, its design influenced by the curves and waves of modernist building, and that, later, Xenakis would use the stochastic systems of mathematical modelling employed by statisticians and economists, should not divert us from the sheer physical excitement of his music. The composer's process may have been intellectual and controlled, but the resulting sounds are visceral. Those masses of instruments move like flocking birds, all in the same broad direction but each with its individual flight path. The slabs of sound thus created are rather volatile on the surface, but function, nonetheless, as large choirs of instruments.

The quintessential sound of *Metastaseis*, and many other pieces by Xenakis, is of two or more of these sonic slabs moving together, either crossing over each other or colliding, and some listeners to his music have inevitably been drawn to consider such occasionally violent music in the context of the composer's biography, in particular his years in the Greek resistance movements: first against the Axis occupation during World War II, then in 1944 against the British imposition of martial law (Xenakis was badly injured and lost an eye). Of course such experiences must play their part in any artist's work, and it was no different for the other musicians discussed in this chapter and in this book: Ustvolskaya spent most of her life in the Soviet Union, her music hidden in a drawer; Webern was partly sympathetic to the Nazi cause, then found his music banned by them; Schoenberg, a Jew, was forced into exile by the Third Reich; and being a black musician in 1950s America, Muddy Waters was obliged to occupy certain seats on buses and in restaurants, enter buildings through certain doors and drink from certain water fountains. How could such experiences fail to affect the music produced by those who endured them?

But art comes from the imagination as much as from experience, and great artists have great imaginations. Sometimes they might be responding to events in their lives, but the imagination can also offer a refuge from such events. And, without wishing to seem mystical, it may also be that age-old traditions of music exert a pull on an artist's imagination that is at least equal to the presence in their life of a Hitler or a Stalin or the Ku Klux Klan.

When I listen to Xenakis's music, it is not images of armed resistance that come to mind. The analogy I have always found hard to resist is of tectonic plates, shaping and reshaping the earth's crust, forming mountain ranges and great valleys. In Xenakis's *Metastaseis*, in Ustvolskaya's Sonata No 6, in Muddy Waters's 'Mannish Boy', in Stravinsky's *Les noces*, in the music of Janáček and in the early recordings of Elvis Presley, I hear music that is in touch with something fundamental in our existence, music that seeks and rediscovers the earthy side of our nature, and in doing so restores and resets our humanity. Precisely because of this, it also puts in motion new cycles of musical creativity that will themselves end up in a return to those same primitive qualities.

2

Understanding the Stone

An interview with Richard Barrett

Richard Barrett (born in Swansea, South Wales, in 1959) is a prolific composer of music that is often loud and muscular. He has written for all manner of musical forces, pieces for solo instruments and for orchestra, but seems most attracted to large ensembles made up of unique combinations of single instruments. Many of these pieces are part of larger series. He works also with electronics, especially in the area of free improvisation. Most of his professional life has been spent in continental Europe. At the time of this interview, conducted via Skype in June 2014, then substantially edited by the composer, he was living in Belgrade.

Andrew Ford: Let's start with your piece *EARTH*. Can you describe the piece and tell me why it's called *EARTH*?

Richard Barrett: *EARTH* is a piece for trombone and percussion from around 1987/1988, so by my standards it's rather ancient now. And that was a time in my mid to late twenties when I was concerned with exploring some basic aspects of what would go on to be central characteristics of my work in general. One point of departure was the idea that you have two instruments with almost nothing in common – one played by blowing, the other by hitting – and more particularly that the sounds they produce can't be merged with one another in any way. So *EARTH* ended up as a series of attempts to bring the instruments together, a sequence of angles of approach that the two instruments take towards each other, ultimately resulting in them coming apart – not only from each other but also within themselves, so that, for example, the trombonist eventually has independent notations for the slide and the lips. On the other hand, one of the ways in which the instruments could form a single whole is through different kinds of rhythmical and structural synchronicity, which is probably one of the most memorable features of the piece.

AF: You've used the word 'ancient' regarding this piece, which is now more that twenty-five years old, but there's also something 'ancient' about the piece, isn't there? I mean, there's something – to my ears, at any rate – that suggests that this piece has been dug up somewhere and that it's some sort of artefact. I know that you've described it as being a kind of invented folk music. What do you mean by that?

RB: If you look at the way rhythmical thinking has evolved in different musical traditions across the globe, you see that the Western classical musical tradition isn't particularly sophisticated in comparison, for example, to Indonesian or South Indian music.

This is just to name two examples of musics I've taken a particular interest in, and which often, if distantly, inform my own work, right up to the percussion trio *urlicht* [2014]. The trombone, of course, is a quintessentially Western instrument – there isn't really anything like it in any other tradition – but percussion instruments are a different matter. With *EARTH*, I was also interested in synthesising percussion sounds by consistently associating instruments with one another, putting the xylophone with its clearly pitched sounds always in unison with a set of woodblocks, so that those clear pitches are, so to speak, unfocused by the woodblocks; or to put it another way, the woodblock sounds are given different and more variegated colours by the xylophone pitches, effectively resulting in a new instrument whose timbral complexity and irregularity might be reminiscent of musical cultures outside the Western classical one.

As for invented folk music – digging the music up, as you put it – that idea has various kinds of resonances in other work of mine, such as a series of compositions entitled *codex*, of which there are currently fourteen. These are rather experimental pieces, which mostly involve taking a combination of notated materials, verbal suggestions and music worked out collaboratively in rehearsals, as a context or a network of focal points for the spontaneous actions of free improvisation in performance. One of the ways in which I've thought of those pieces – maybe you can see this as a development of what happens in *EARTH* – is as the fragmentary remains of some sort of musical civilisation distant in time or space, which we then have to reconstruct. Ancient Greek music, for instance, has been successfully performed by a number of groups in the last few decades, based on very fragmentary and sparsely notated materials, evidence of performance, iconography of the instruments and so forth. I became interested also in the idea of taking something which is incomplete in that sort of way, which seems like it has survived some event which destroyed most of the civilisation from which it arose, as a stimulus, an inspiration for inventing something new.

AF: You mentioned that Western classical music isn't, on the whole, very adventurous rhythmically, and certainly not by comparison to the music of Indonesia or southern India. What Western classical music has a lot of, of course, is harmony, which most other music does not – or not at all in the same way. Would you say that your own music, therefore, has been less interested in harmony and more interested in rhythm, and certainly more interested in timbre?

RB: Yes, in so far as there's a hard and fast distinction between those things, which fundamentally I don't think there is. Not having gone through the pathway of a formal or institutional musical education meant that I could make the choice of whether, and to what extent, the Western classical tradition would actually play a role in my own musical evolution. I think that, as a result, I have chosen not to see it as some sort of central point from which everything else emanates, but as a point in a constellation where the balance between the elements is constantly changing.

What does this mean in terms of harmony? I suppose that my attitude towards harmony is a little bit like . . . well, it's a language that I've learnt, but it's not my native language, so to speak. And I would compare that with, for example, the way that a lot of the writings of Samuel Beckett were written in French, which was not his native language. When he was asked about this at one point he said it made it easier for him to write 'without style', by which I think he meant without feeling the kind of influences that a 'mother tongue' inevitably exerts, influences so deep-seated that it might be impossible to become consciously aware of them, and thereby to get beyond them or to see them for what they were. By 'without style' he doesn't mean without personality – his writings in French are extremely individual – but that every word had to be consciously *chosen* in a way that, in one's native language, it wouldn't have to be.

AF: But in the process you invent a new style, don't you? I'm thinking now of the novelist Joseph Conrad, who was Polish and yet is regarded as one of the great English stylists; and it's partly because he was Polish that he produced this distinctive style in English. And the same, I'm sure, is true of Beckett in French. So you can't avoid style, much as you may try. But maybe it's just something you don't think about?

RB: I think that it's very important when evolving as an artist to become as consciously aware as possible of all of the inputs, influences, conditioning that go into the music, and then to be in a position to accept or reject them. To use them, to develop them, or to observe them from a distance, so to speak. So Conrad is a good example. Nabokov is another example of somebody who developed a very individual style, yet did so in a language that he wouldn't originally have chosen.

AF: Staying with words, the texts you have worked with in your music have tended to be dark, despairing, even apocalyptic. You mentioned Beckett; we should mention Paul Celan, Euripides's *Women of Troy*. More recently, there's been Hölderlin. You might find this surprising, and perhaps you don't agree, but I feel your body of work in general is optimistic in outlook – not least in terms of its sheer abundance; I mean, there's a lot of it. Does some of your music come out of the tension between despair, on the one hand, and creativity, on the other? Is it, in fact, that Beckett line: 'I can't go on, I'll go on'?

RB: That's maybe one aspect of it, but it isn't the only one. As a socialist, I am of course convinced that people are capable of creating a society based on justice and equality. That would make me a great deal more optimistic in my outlook than many composers who are creating more superficially 'optimistic' music than mine! The fact that I do 'go on', that the work continues the attempt to search outward as well as inward for new discoveries, new forms, connections, possibilities – or at least I feel that it does – is surely evidence of a fundamentally hopeful view of the potential of the human imagination, in composition, performance *and* listening. More than that would be superfluous. If you'd asked me that question twenty or more years ago I would probably have answered it differently; it's not that my attitude has become more optimistic over the years, but that I've realised something deeper about what I've been doing and why. On the other hand, I think it's clear that we're also capable of destroying each other and everything else, in the absence of a more widespread shift in consciousness.

AF: You have written a lot of music for non-conventional ensembles, and I'd like to come back to the question of harmony here. As far as John Cage was concerned, harmony was a matter of bringing sounds together, not a matter of specific pitches. And in your pieces you're always bringing sounds together, and you bring them together in a way that puts the actual nature of those sounds at the forefront of the listening experience – it becomes something that is quite visceral. And I'm wondering if this is something which you consciously do, or again, whether it's the result of concentrating on certain aspects of your technique and not on others.

RB: Cage's work seems to become more important to me as time goes on. Recently I was giving a series of talks about composition and performance in which I mentioned his music rather often, and someone asked me who my most important influences are – 'apart from Cage, that is'. And actually this is something else I now recognise as having been present in my ways of making music from the very start. However, I think the phenomenon you're talking about has maybe more to do with the influence on instrumental music of my work with electronics.

One of the things that fascinates me about that medium is the way that spontaneously conceived combinations of sound-materials, perhaps of widely differing nature and origin, can set in motion a kind of quasi-alchemical reaction, producing something quite different from the individual components it consists of. I think this has a very clear impact on the way that I approach instrumental writing.

For example, let's look at the beginning of a piece from the 1990s, *negatives* [1988–93]. There's a unison pitch – an F, in fact, which occurs at the beginnings of my compositions more often than not – played by a very disparate collection of instruments: an angklung (an Indonesian, bamboo-rattle-based instrument), sitar, flute, trombone, ten-string acoustic guitar and a quartet of bowed strings. Each of these exists in its own intonational world, so that a traditional kind of blended unison isn't really possible – the expanded concept of unison here is neither a single sound nor a layering of discrete sounds but something else, which I think is relatable to composing directly with sounds in the electronic domain, as well as to examples like Stockhausen's *Gruppen*, which is constantly shifting in perspective between discrete and textural sound (and which itself was crucially conditioned by discoveries in the new world of electronic music).

AF: When you use the angklung or the sitar, of course you're not doing it because these instruments are Indonesian or Indian. The music doesn't sound Indonesian or Indian any more than your use of the Hardanger fiddle makes your music sound Norwegian or your use of the koto makes it sound Japanese. You're throwing them in there, in a way, to disrupt the sound of the Western classical instruments, and to produce new and previously unimagined combinations of sound colours.

RB: Many of the playing methods used, for example, in the string instruments of China or Japan would, in terms of Western music, be described as extended playing techniques: scraping the strings, harmonics, *sul ponticello* [bowing or plucking a string on or near the bridge] and so on, which are relatively new as musical materials in Western music but which elsewhere have been around for hundreds of years. There's not the distinction you have even in a lot of contemporary music for Western instruments between the 'central' and 'marginal' sounds an instrument can make, and this feature has also informed the way I think about the Western instrumentarium. In other words, the non-Western instruments expand further upon an already expanded view of instrumentalism applied to the Western ones. As you imply, it doesn't make the music sound Eastern or whatever, it isn't a question of confronting the European tradition with some kind of 'other' but of opening up new forms of timbral (and harmonic!) heterogeneity. I don't think of it so much in terms of taking Western music as the paradigm and disrupting it with something else, but I would see it more in terms of changing everything so as to create a musical space where they can all belong together.

This has a parallel for me with the performance of freely impro-vised music. Every different collaboration that I take part in, including working with people I'd never even heard before we go on stage together, should change me in some way, should cause me to do things in a way I haven't done them in other situations, as a contribution to the composite personality which is collectively composing the music. This is one of the aspects of the music I find most rewarding, also with long-time collaborations, not just as a performer but also as a listener, and I would think other listeners might feel the same way. Returning to the combination of instru-ments from different traditions, each component thus has a new kind of environment to work in, which changes and expands the character of *every* instrument, so that what we end up with is not a combination of different pre-existing worlds but actually yet another world.

AF: Do you see composition and improvisation as broadly the same thing, only that improvisation is faster?

RB: I regard composition as applying to any form of creative music, and of improvisation as one *method* of creating, which is charac-terised, as you say, by speed to a certain extent, although of course every performative and compositional experience one has had feeds in some way into each new performance. Instrumentalism, struc-tural thinking, expressive compulsions – all of the things that go into notated composition – also go into improvisation. My reali-sation, about ten or twelve years ago, that improvisation is a method of composition, no more and no less, might not seem like such a big deal, but it had a decisive effect on the course my musical thinking has taken since then, in the domain of notated composition as well as others. Improvised music goes right back to the beginnings of my musical activity. I've come to think of myself as basically an improvising musician in whom a strong commitment to notated composition has developed, rather than the other way around.

AF: Well, it also seems to me, listening to your music (I mean your composed music), that it's so physical, that for you to have this other life as somebody that makes the sounds yourself and makes them here and now and sends them out into the world, is probably significant. It's part of your makeup as a composer – that you get physical too.

RB: This may sound strange, given that I'm so involved with highly systematised compositional methods, but these techniques for me are there in order to create 'instruments' I can respond to spontaneously. I want to create the conditions where the potential of sudden insight can be made fruitful. This isn't a position I've taken for the sake of it but something which reflects my experience as a listener and which I hope to encourage in other listeners.

One of the things I might systematise, for example, is the order in which I compose the cells or segments of a composition, not arbitrarily but as an essential part of the evolution of the music's expressive and structural identity. I would then randomise the order in which I complete the composition of those segments. I might start off somewhere in the middle, with empty spaces before and after, above and below, and as the random filling-in of the mosaic proceeds I begin to have to make connections between segments in any or all directions. An improvisation also evolves as a moving point between the memory of what *has* happened, the perception of what *is* happening and the anticipation of what *might* happen – except there, of course, you don't have that spatialisation of time which is afforded by a score, enabling you to go back and forth in time and in any other direction, independently of the way time will ultimately be experienced in listening. I'm taking advantage, in other words, of that opportunity in order not just to tell the story of how the music was made but to create another kind of structural dimension that isn't idiomatic to improvised music.

AF: Let's come back to the earth and talk about Andy Goldsworthy, because he's an artist whose 'earth art' I've admired for many years, and I know that you have too. And I know also that you have come up with a musical response in the form of music for cello and electronics – a piece called *life-form* [2011–12]. I wonder whether, in doing that, you actually tried to find some sort of musical equivalent for the way in which Andy Goldsworthy works in and with earth?

RB: I always have the feeling when I'm working with electronic music that I'm exploring an unfamiliar world, as if walking along a beach of infinite length, picking up pebbles and at one point thinking, Yes, I can do something with this, which immediately starts to focus my mind on what kinds of pebbles I'm interested in, at that particular moment, helping me to decide whether the next pebble I find is going to form part of whatever it is I'm doing. And actually working on instrumental music isn't so different, although it's maybe on a less tangible kind of level. So this feeling of discovering rather than inventing the materials, and of discovering the connections between materials on the basis of some kind of structure or vision which gradually comes into view as the materials are assembled, has often reminded me of how I imagine Goldsworthy goes about his work.

One of the things he talks about in his film *Rivers and Tides* – which I recommend that everyone interested in musical composition should see at some point – is in terms of 'understanding the stone'. That is to say, his understanding of the materials that he's working with emerges in the course of working with them, and if he hasn't understood the stone completely then the structure he's building is going to fall apart before it's finished. And so what is expressed by the freestanding, pinecone-like structure made out of flat stones, or whatever it happens to be, is indeed the understanding of the stone, without which it wouldn't be possible to conceive of that shape and to realise it.

My understanding of *my* materials, then, is what a listener might experience as an integrity and coherence in sound – for example, the kind of unstable balance I mentioned in connection with *Gruppen* between an overall texture and the discrete sounds within it. And to that extent also, these electronic materials I'm working with do resemble natural phenomena: they combine extreme simplicity with extreme complexity a lot of the time, and that, I think, is something that my music as a whole does.

One objection that might be raised to my comparison with Goldsworthy is that what I'm doing is sitting at a computer and creating synthetic sounds out of numbers – rather paradoxically, I was drawn towards using only synthetic sounds in the electronic part of *life-form*, rather than the recorded and transformed sounds I've used previously in my electronic music. But somehow it seemed appropriate in this case, that the sounds should be 'grown' from first principles. Actually, there is one exception to this, a little anecdotal, I suppose, but there's one section in the piece where you can hear cowbells in the distance, and these cowbells were recorded in France outside the house of Arne Deforce, the cellist I was writing the piece for. And of course this shows the influence of Gustav Mahler, another composer whose music often traverses extremes of complexity and simplicity, who would use cowbells in his symphonies in expressively and structurally very similar kinds of moments.

AF: And off in the distance.

RB: Yes. So what I was going to say was that one might object that the way I composed *life-form* was rather artificial, whereas Goldsworthy of course is using leaves and thorns and so on, but his interventions into nature are also, in a different way, blurring the distinction between the natural and the artificial. And that, I think, is very much at the heart of what we're talking about here, with the physical and visceral nature of music, the examples of Cage and Mahler as well as Goldsworthy. That which is made by human hands and that which isn't can be interwoven to the point that it isn't always possible to tell where one ends and the other starts.

3

Dance of the Earth

Rhythm is all. Where there is rhythm, there is music.
Handwritten by Igor Stravinsky at the
head of 'Dance of the Earth' in his own
'choreographic libretto' of *The Rite of Spring*

When music goes primitive, often enough it inspires dancing. We see this very clearly in popular music, particularly rock and roll. The more that music is concerned with rhythm rather than harmony or melody or lyrics, the more it makes us want to move. Early rock and roll, with its heavy back beat (the second and fourth beats of a 4/4 metre), grounded the music on the dance floor, and that is where it seems bound always to return. As Chuck Berry sang in his hymn of praise to rock and roll music, 'It's got a back beat, you can't lose it / Any old time you use it . . .'

In fact, so ubiquitous was the rock and roll back beat that anything which diverged from it was instantly noticeable. So a figure such as Bo Diddley always stood slightly apart. His songs typically used a rhythmic template that was highly syncopated, not sounding the second and third beats at all, but instead playing the off beats that might be added on top of a standard 4/4 by a cowbell or claves. So distinctive was this rhythm that it became known as the 'Bo Diddley beat'. Buddy Holly and later the Rolling Stones used it, on 'Not Fade Away', as did the Strangeloves, on 'I Want Candy'. But it was above all highly danceable music, and whenever rock has moved away from that into something more exploratory, more multilayered, less beat-driven, the next turn of the wheel has always brought it back to dance.

The Beatles, to take a clear and, perhaps, rather obvious example, went from the dance music of *Please Please Me* (1963) to the sit-down-and-listen songs of *Sgt Pepper's Lonely Hearts Club Band* in a mere four years (it is significant that *Sgt Pepper* was the first pop album to come with printed song lyrics), and thereafter, particularly on *Abbey Road* and *Let It Be*, attempted to return to something they felt had been lost. The single 'Get Back' was emblematic of that search; significantly, you could dance to it as you hadn't been able to dance to much of *Sgt Pepper*.

When punk pricked the pompous bubble of 'progressive rock' in the mid-1970s, it was with music so rhythmically and harmonically basic that the dancing it inspired involved simply jumping up and down. Film of young people with safety pins in their lips and eyebrows, pogoing energetically at a club in the King's Road, Chelsea, while the Sex Pistols perform on stage, may today appear comic – most old dance crazes do – but it encapsulates, rather neatly, the connection between basic music, particularly basic rhythm, and dance.

For centuries, new dances and forms of popular music have nearly always emerged from the lower classes, so that when composers have sought more primitive and rhythmic modes of musical expression, particularly when they have drawn on folk-loric or other popular culture, dance steps have often been attached. Those bourrées and gigues in the suites of Handel and Bach, the minuets in the symphonies and sonatas of Haydn and Mozart, Chopin's waltzes, Mahler's Ländlers, Debussy's cake-walks, Ástor Piazzolla's tangos and Matthew Hindson's rave pieces: all are examples of composers refreshing their music by using dance styles of the day or of the recent past, and in every case, with the possible exception of the minuet, those dance styles had lowly origins. In refreshing their art, the composers were also admitting the demotic and, particularly, the corporeal. They were aiming their music as much at the body as the mind.

There is a parallel here with music for the stage. While West-ern art music may seem to be based in the concert hall – at least since the modern concert hall's invention two centuries ago – many of its boldest and most far-reaching innovations have occurred in the theatre, in operas and ballets. If we say Western music's greatest stylistic innovators have been Monteverdi, Beet-hoven, Wagner and Stravinsky (and of course that is arguable), then Beethoven stands apart in that his one opera, *Fidelio*, is more a summing up and fleshing out of his musical style than its source. For the others, the theatre was their crucible. The musical discov-eries of Monteverdi and Wagner both had enormous ramifica-tions for what came next, and each composer was, above all, a man of the theatre, his musical innovations serving dramatic needs. (We could make the list a little longer by adding the names of Mozart, Berlioz, Tchaikovsky, Verdi, Berg and Philip Glass:

all composers for the theatre.)

For Stravinsky, like Tchaikovsky before him, dance was the primary driver of innovation, and in his case the inspirer of some of the twentieth century's most important musical works: *Les noces*, *Pulcinella*, *Apollo*, *The Fairy's Kiss* and *Agon* span not only three decades in the middle of the twentieth century, but also three of their composer's (and therefore the century's) most important stylistic developments. If *Les noces* was the apotheosis of Stravinsky's rhythmically vital, Russian-folklore style, then *Pulcinella* (1920) – composed after it, though premiered in advance – is the start of thirty years of neo-classicism. *Apollo* (1928) is neo-classicism at its coolest, and *The Fairy's Kiss* (1928) neo-classicism at its most magical – in some senses it is almost neo-Romantic, since it looks back to Tchaikovsky. Finally, *Agon* (1957), with its mix of chutzpah, insouciance and grit, fuses neo-classicism with serial technique. They are all great works.

But it is Stravinsky's three early ballets, *The Firebird* (1910), *Petrushka* (1911) and *The Rite of Spring*, that remain their composer's most famous and most performed scores, in and especially out of the theatre. All were commissioned for Diaghilev's Ballets Russes (as were *Les noces* and *Pulcinella*), all were seminal scores of the early twentieth century, and all were inextricably connected to the human body. But *The Rite of Spring* is recognised as one of the most important works of Western music, and one of its most notorious.

* * *

It was always going to be notorious. The Paris seasons of the Ballets Russes had a reputation for their ability to produce a *succès de scandale*. In 1912, a year to the day before the premiere of *The Rite*, Vaslav Nijinsky had created the role of the faun in a short ballet, *L'après-midi d'un faune* ('The Afternoon of a Faun'), inspired by Stéphane Mallarmé's symbolist poem of the same name and danced to Debussy's orchestral score, *Prélude à l'après-midi d'un faune* (1894). In addition to dancing the main role, Nijinsky also made his debut as a choreographer. While there was ample justification for what the audience witnessed in both the music and (particularly) the poem, still the sight of Nijinsky miming masturbation with a silk scarf at the ballet's climax shocked a lot of people.

'Astonish me,' Diaghilev liked to tell his artists, and they regularly did. With Stravinsky's music, Roerich's scenario and designs, and Nijinsky's choreography, *The Rite of Spring* had the most widely reported opening night in history. On stage, a sacrificial virgin danced herself to death; from the orchestra pit came music of unprecedented violence; and in the stalls of Paris's newly opened Théâtre des Champs-Elysées a small riot broke out. This was on 29 May 1913. Ever since, the score has been regarded as landmark in cultural provocation, later generations of composers hearing in the pugnaciousness of the score a manifesto for artistic courage and dogged will.

In recent years, some revisionists have tried to tell us that the first-night riot did not really occur, or, if it did, that it was a put-up job, staged to bolster the company's or the composer's reputation.

But there are too many eye-witness accounts to dismiss the story. It's perfectly true that the shouting, hissing and fisticuffs gained Stravinsky some welcome publicity, but it is equally true that many in the audience were genuinely outraged by their first encounter with *The Rite*.

Even Diaghilev felt confronted by the music the first time he heard it. Stravinsky sat at a piano and played the impresario that section known as 'The Augurs of Spring', a single, dissonant chord – a combination of F flat major and E flat dominant seventh – repeating steadily more than two hundred times, the only variation coming from an accented attack, now on the beat, now off it, that creates syncopation – and thus a sense of momentum – while simultaneously emphasising the harmonic monotony.

'Will it go on like this for long?' Diaghilev shouted as Stravinsky hammered out the chords.

'Till the end, my dear,' the offended composer shouted back.

Diaghilev must have known at once that he had another *scandale* on his hands, and it is surely no accident that when he programmed the premiere, he placed *The Rite* immediately after the Romantic ballet, *Les sylphides*, danced to a selection of pieces by Chopin. The contrast could hardly have been greater.

The Rite of Spring begins with a high solo bassoon. At the premiere, the curtain remained down through the introduction, so that the audience was obliged to give its full attention to the music, and so unusual was the sound of the high bassoon that musicians in the audience began to debate its identity. Was it a saxophone?

Was it a cor anglais? Was it, perhaps, two instruments doubling the same line? The player must have been terrified. Bassoon solos were not so very common in orchestral music; completely exposed bassoon solos – with no other instruments playing at all – were unheard of; and exposed bassoon solos at the very top of the instrument's range in the first bar of the piece must still be considered extreme.

Of course, a century on, this moment has become a bassoonist's party piece, robbing it of a degree of its power. The tension that Stravinsky sought to generate – partly through the player's nerves – is hard to replicate. Harrison Birtwistle once joked that in order to preserve the tension of the opening, the score might be transposed up a semitone each year.

The bassoon is swiftly joined by other wind instruments – a French horn, a clarinet and bass clarinet, a piccolo clarinet, then a cor anglais and two more bassoons – in a growing tangle of counterpoint. To modern ears, this music sounds rather seductive, but to an audience unfamiliar with it – an audience that had just been listening to a Chopin waltz – it was impenetrably complex. Animated commentary from the patrons in the stalls (and others' attempts to hush it) had already begun to obscure much of the musical detail when the curtain finally rose.

According to the composer, this was when all hell broke loose. The audience saw what Stravinsky called 'a group of knock-kneed and long-braided lolitas jumping up and down' in time to the stamping chord of the 'The Augurs of Spring'. Soon the dancers on stage could no longer hear the music above the shouted abuse from the auditorium. Stravinsky said he was 'never again . . . that angry', and yet he must have known that this would be the making of him. And it didn't take long, either: only a month later, following a concert performance of the music alone, the composer was cheered to the echo and carried from the hall on the shoulders of his supporters.

Almost certainly, what that first-night crowd objected to was exactly what the later one found so exciting, and what still excites and occasionally upsets audiences today: Stravinsky's engagement with brutality, his summoning of primitive musical urges, his roughing up of that sleek and sophisticated organism, the symphony orchestra. He did this in a variety of ways, but folk music was at the heart of it. The cosmopolitan composer, who had already left Russia for good, liked to play down his cultural roots. It is true that, late in life, he discussed the origins of *The Rite of Spring* by referring to childhood memories of melting ice on the lakes near Saint Petersburg cracking loudly, but he always denied that there were any traditional melodies in the score. Now we know that the piece is full of folk tunes, because the American musicologist Richard Taruskin has identified them. Even that opening bassoon solo is a version of a folk song from Lithuania.

However, it is not the tunes that shock in *The Rite of Spring* so much as the sound world of the music, rhythmic, harmonic and timbral. It is debatable how much detail the members of that first-night audience would have discerned amid the din of protest, but assuming they heard some of it, and that they already knew Stravinsky's previous work for Diaghilev – *The Firebird* and

Petrushka – they would, in part, have been responding to an orchestral sound that was considerably less alluring, less *glittering* than those of his earlier works. Those scores – one a fairy-tale ballet in the Tchaikovsky mould, the other the tale of a puppet come to life – made use of tuned percussion, such as xylophones and glockenspiels, as well as orchestral pianos, celestas and harps (no fewer than three of them in *The Firebird*). None of these instruments appears in *The Rite of Spring*.

In their place, percussionists play a limited range of non-tuned instruments: a bass drum, a tam-tam (a large gong), a tambourine and a rasping Latin-American güiro, often replaced in performance by a washboard played with thimbles for extra volume. Then, raised up and seated behind matching sets of kettle drums, there are two timpanists – a rare sight in the concert hall, and unheard of in the ballet pit. Equally unusual are the orchestra's eight horns (instead of the usual four) and two bass tubas. French horns are normally played with their bells facing backwards, the player's right hand resting inside the bell, but at various points in *The Rite* Stravinsky had put the words 'Les pavillions en l'air' in the horn parts, instructing the players to turn their instruments upside down, raising their bells high in the air for maximum volume and, if they can be seen by the audience, maximum show. The rest of the orchestra is correspondingly larger, with five each of the woodwinds (the usual number is three) and five trumpets, including a bass trumpet.

Stravinsky used his orchestra with originality and resourcefulness, its job to reveal and reinforce his rhythmic invention. The stamping chords of 'The Augurs of Spring', with their accented syncopations, are played by the strings (all down-bows), while the accents are delivered by the eight horns. Everything is in the mid-range, the sound almost drab; there is nothing sensational about it. Like the unchanging chord, it is monotonous, yet at the same time somehow threatening. The stamping chord, with its syncopations, quickly became the signature sound of *The Rite*, and this was doubtless helped twenty-seven years later by Walt Disney's addition of dinosaurs in his celebrated *Fantasia* (1940). But Stravinsky recognised the power of this moment right from the start, for he used elements of it throughout the score, and especially in the culmination of the first part of the piece, 'Dance of the Earth'.

There is a great urgency to this section, a race-against-time quality. The tempo indication is *prestissimo*, with a metronome marking of 168 crotchets (quarter notes) to the minute. Throughout, the strings and timpani play scurrying semiquavers (sixteenth notes), intermittently encouraged by the trumpets. Against this, the horns and bass drum have triplet quavers, so that the entire dance occurs above a rhythmic ostinato of three against four. It forms a continuum – like the persistent stamping of 'The Augurs of Spring' – and at the start and end of 'Dance of the Earth' it is spiked by accents played by high woodwind and trumpets in the same proportion as the syncopated accents in 'The Augurs'. There is a further connection between the two sections in the way that the rhythmic continuum of 'Dance of the Earth' is underlined by an unvaried harmonic device. It is another aspect of the composer's desire to be primitive. Centuries of Western music had been founded on harmonic change and homecoming, but here, as in

'The Augurs', and indeed in the final 'Sacrificial Dance', the harmony of 'Dance of the Earth' does not move at all – it employs a single chord.

Since the sixteenth century, Western art music had been heading for the home key – the tonic, or a version of it. The sound of a perfect cadence – dominant to tonic, or V–I – was how you knew a piece was over. In Beethoven's fifth symphony, to take an extreme example, the finale seems designed to celebrate the triumphant arrival in C major of a C minor symphony. The music of the coda rushes ahead in a manner not wholly dissimilar to 'Dance of the Earth', before reaching the tonic C via its dominant G. There's nothing unusual about this, except for the composer's insistence on the moment: over and over, Beethoven takes us from the dominant G to the tonic C, finally slamming the music into the home key and remaining there for a series of defiant full stops.

That's one way to do it. Another, subtler way is Wagner's in *Tristan und Isolde*. Here the composer approaches the tonic circuitously and very slowly – over the entire four-and-a-half-hour length of the opera, you might argue – and one feels an overwhelming relief when the tonic B major is finally established. But whether the arrival in the home key induces feelings of triumph or relief, the sense of finality is palpable. This does not happen in *The Rite of Spring*.

In 'Dance of the Earth', the harmonic stasis is a study in primitivism, the violent junking of a system of keys focusing our attention on timbre and, above all, on rhythm. A comparison with Schoenberg's newly adopted atonality is instructive, for when the composers of the second Viennese school abandoned tonality, they did so by gradually expanding the chromatic harmonies of German Romanticism. Indeed, you might think of a work such as Schoenberg's second string quartet as post-tonal. Stravinsky's 'Dance of the Earth', in contrast, is pre-tonal; it is as though tonality never existed. For this whole section of *The Rite*, save a few bars, the double basses sound a C natural – in effect, a drone – while also executing a whole-tone scale starting on F sharp. This ascending six-note scale (F sharp, G sharp, B flat, C, D, E) is doubled by the lower woodwind and, later, the low brass; like the stamping of 'The Augurs', it continues 'to the end, my dear'.

A whole-tone scale is ambiguous because it has no root position; every note is of equal importance, unless the music around it chooses to emphasise one of them. The double basses' C natural fulfils this function, though it would be misleading to describe the music as being 'in' C. The repeating scales lead nowhere except back to their beginning – there can be no sense of harmonic movement, as there is in the Beethoven and Wagner examples – and, when the music stops, it is as though we are left hurtling through midair. It is one of the most shocking/thrilling moments in *The Rite*.

There are two major differences between the end of Part One of *The Rite of Spring* and the end of Part Two. One is the intense syncopation of the latter, and the other is the requirement for a musical full stop; the composer presumably reasoned that after half an hour of drama, the music could not simply cease – it required a real ending. The syncopation in the 'Sacrificial Dance' is one of the great innovations of *The Rite*. Instead of the regular stamping of 'The Augurs of Spring' or the endless semiquavers of 'Dance of the Earth', syncopated and thus animated by the placing of accents, now the whole orchestra becomes convulsed in syncopation. There had been changing metres in music before, but nothing to compare with a passage that contains time signatures of 3/16, 2/16, 2/8 and 5/16, alternating from bar to bar. When you factor in the tempo, which is quick – at least 126 quavers (eighth notes) to the minute – you have music that is always off-balance, toppling forwards, music of unprecedented volatility.

Except for the harmony. Because, as with 'The Augurs' and 'Dance of the Earth', the harmony of the 'Sacrificial Dance' is static. You could play that high-energy music with its constantly shifting metres above an unchanging drone, and indeed that is what the double basses set up, oscillating between A and C for the duration. As the virgin dances towards her death on stage, Stravinsky ratchets up the tension, giving us music that is dynamically animated in terms of tempo, metre and rhythm, but harmonically trapped and incapable of transformation. While the girl dances, she lives; but she cannot escape her fate. And, like the doomed virgin, the music must just keep on repeating until it stops dead. In 'Dance of the Earth' it was enough to do only this, to stop in midair. But now, at the very end, the piece needs something more, and what Stravinsky offers is the major disappointment of *The Rite*.

There's a loud chord, a soft, high tremolo in the violins, a gentle rising figure in the flutes, a silence, then two more chords, high and low – wham, bam. The gesture is too obvious, the effect perfunctory, even a little cheap. The piece ends on D, intended as the tonic after all those As and Cs, but that is not how it feels. Occasionally, a conductor can time the chords so as to create a frisson of surprise, but usually the end of the piece just falls a bit flat. And the composer must have known he had not got it right, because following the work's premiere, Stravinsky continued to make small adjustments and revisions to his score, and especially to the final part. Indeed, he was still changing things as late as 1967, more than half a century after the piece was first played.

But the reason the ending doesn't come off is that the music leading up to it is so extraordinary (still), so insistent yet so thrillingly unstable that it makes a convincing final bar all but impossible.

Stravinsky's grand musical construction is ultimately a contradiction. The scale of the music and of its emotional impact mark out *The Rite of Spring* as a final hurrah of late Romanticism. It demands a grand ending. But its simultaneous rejection of Romanticism, evident in the studied barbarism of its musical fabric and its rejection of harmonic goals, rules out any such conclusion. At the last, the piece trips itself up, and despite the composer's inveterate tinkering with the score, it always will.

Ultimately, *The Rite* is a rejection of Romanticism. It is the musical equivalent of cubism. It confronts us like the sullen whores in Picasso's 'Les demoiselles d'Avignon', their faces morphing into primitive masks as they meet our eyes with their unflinching stares. It is a harbinger of the years of mass killing about to afflict Europe. It was, and in some sense still is, 'the shock of the new'. These judgements may be glib, but they still seem broadly correct.

* * *

72

The premiere of *The Rite of Spring* is such a big moment in the history of Western music that the music has spawned numerous imitations, tributes and other works that find themselves compared to Stravinsky's score simply because they are loud or syncopated or contain moments of musical violence. Two of the earliest came from opposite sides of the global political divide.

Shortly after his arrival in New York City in 1915, the French-born composer Edgard Varèse (1883–1965) commenced work on what would be his largest orchestral work, *Amériques*, full of the noise of his new home, right down to the police sirens. The score shows the influence of *The Rite*, from the gentle, rather pastoral flute of its opening pages to the relentless smashing of its climaxes. And while it might seem, from its title, like a Frenchman's musical response to the New World, and is surely that to some degree, Varèse would not have been unhappy with the description 'primitive'. Where Stravinsky often seemed to resent his origins, Varèse would insist to his death that he was still, at heart, a Burgundian peasant.

He completed *Amériques* in 1921, revising it six years later. This was the same year that the young Alexander Mosolov (1900–73) composed his brief, though no less barbaric, tone-poem *Zavod* or *The Iron Foundry*. A hymn of praise – not of nature or pagan rites, but of the Soviet machine – it was composed at a moment in history when revolutionary attitudes in the arts were still welcomed in the new Russia; this, of course, would not last.

Other examples of works inspired by *The Rite* might be Gustav Holst's *The Planets* (1914–16), particularly 'Mars – the bringer of war' and 'Uranus – the magician' with its double timpani action; Percy Grainger's *The Warriors* (1913–22); George Antheil's *Ballet mécanique* (1923) and *Sonata sauvage* (1923); Silvestre Revueltas's *Sensemayá* (1938); Charles Koechlin's *Les Bandar-log* (1940), Antill's *Corroboree*, Xenakis's *Terretektorh* (1965), Alberto Ginastera's *Popol Vuh* ('The Creation of the World', 1975–83) and Harrison Birtwistle's *Earth Dances* (1986). There is, indeed, a whole subcategory of works that have the earth in their titles, including Brian Ferneyhough's *La terre est un homme* ('The Earth Is a Man', 1979), Peter Sculthorpe's *Earth Cry* (1986), Michael Finnissy's *Red Earth* (1988) and Tan Dun's *Earth Concerto* (2009).

Not all these composers acknowledged a debt to Stravinsky. Like his compatriot Antill, Grainger denied ever having heard *The Rite of Spring* when he began work on *The Warriors*, though he was in London at the time of the Ballets Russes' visit in 1913, a few weeks after the premiere, and following his death a ticket to a performance was found among his papers. And while each might exhibit primitivist tendencies, by no means are all these pieces studies in barbarism. Koechlin's *Les Bandar-log* is a surreal spoof, while in Sculthorpe's *Earth Cry* the primitivism is largely a matter of long-held pedal points and a kind of naive lyricism.

Real savagery in the Western concert hall (or ballet theatre) remains elusive, and this is partly because works of art tend to seek some degree of balance. You can find barbaric moments in large-scale pieces, or wholly barbaric miniatures such as Mosolov's three-minute *Zavod* or Bartók's piano study *Allegro barbaro* (1911), but to be barbarous or violent or aggressive or even simply noisy for any length of time is not only going to result in music that is hard to listen to, but it will also produce diminishing returns. After all, if you are hoping to shock your audience, you require a degree of surprise, so there must be some stretches in a piece of music that contrast with the aggressive bits.

We tend to remember *The Rite of Spring* as half an hour of noisy barbarism, but in fact the piece is much more than that. For one thing, there are passages, such as the opening of Part Two, that are glacially calm. The composer Oliver Knussen once insisted that this section of the piece reflected the early-morning view of Lake Geneva from the window of Stravinsky's work room, and perhaps he was right.

But of course it follows the 'Dance of the Earth', and so there is an uneasiness about this calm. We are waiting for something to happen, and like a great director of suspense films, Stravinsky prolongs the calm to increase our unease, supplying hints of what might be coming. There are little dissonant duets between solo trumpets, flickers of colour from the violins, but nothing really to prepare us for the *accelerando* that turns the French horns, abruptly, into hunting horns, whooping alarmingly, before four timpani and a bass drum pound out eleven beats of unprovoked savagery.

And this is genuine savagery. On the whole, *The Rite* is a sophisticated aping of violence – Debussy called it 'barbarism with all modern conveniences' – but this pounding, at least, is the real thing, and all the more shocking for it.

4

A Poor Music

AN INTERVIEW WITH MARTIN BRESNICK

Martin Bresnick (born in New York City in 1946) has had a double career as teacher and composer. Many of America's best-known younger and middle-generation composers have sat in Bresnick's classes at Yale, including the three founders of Bang on a Can, Michael Gordon, David Lang and Julia Wolfe. But, for Bresnick, composing is the main thing. He has written for all media, from opera to film, and from songs and chamber music to orchestral works. Some of his chamber music falls into a subcategory that he calls 'Opere della musica povera' – 'Works of a poor music'. This interview took place in Sydney in April 2013, with some later tidying up and a few supplementary questions by email. With the centenary of The Rite of Spring *approaching, we began by talking about that work and Bresnick's ambivalent feelings towards it.*

MARTIN BRESNICK: Although I admire *The Rite of Spring*, it's by far not my favourite Stravinsky. I don't think it's as important as people think it is. I think if you look at what was happening between 1910 and 1913, there are many other works that are influential – and certainly in my own musical world *more* influential. On the other hand, I will say without shame that one of the most amazing experiences of my life was hearing Pierre Boulez conduct *The Rite of Spring* with the BBC Symphony Orchestra when I was a young student in Vienna. I was completely captivated by that performance. It was as if Boulez had taken the work apart and reassembled it for us from a composer's point of view. I count that performance as one of the highlights of my listening life.

Nevertheless, that being said, it's a piece that is really a ballet. Also it's assembled from folk tunes, many of them already in Rimsky. Its orchestration is huge and overweights its economic logic – it's this immense Straussian, *Alpine Symphony* kind of orchestra. And from a formal standpoint, you can't ask of it that it be a logical work like, say, Bartók's *Bluebeard's Castle* or Schoenberg's *Pierrot lunaire* – it doesn't work formally in that way. For me as a composer, it is the interplay between formal structures, and the architectonics of those structures in relationship to the substance of music, that constitutes the powerful and memorable part of music to me. So as a sensory experience, yes, *The Rite of Spring* is a knockout. You know, you're knocked on your heels, no doubt about it: Stravinsky intended it and Stravinsky succeeded. But from other perspectives, there are so many other pieces from 1910 to 1913 . . .

So I won't take *The Rite of Spring* on my desert island. I'll take *Jeux* of Debussy, I'll take *Bluebeard's Castle*, I'll take *Pierrot lunaire*, and frankly there are other pieces by Stravinsky I would take that were at least nascent in that period, like *Les noces* and

The Soldier's Tale. Now that I'm thinking about it, there are numerous pieces of Ives from that period that I would also wonder about longer – the third and the fourth symphonies, for example, though the third is probably earlier. And look, shall we leave out the works of Janáček from the same period? Not from my reservoir of musical memories! But that's just me, Andy. One man's opinion. That's why there are horse races.

ANDREW FORD: When you think of *The Rite of Spring*, what do you think of first? Is it a sound? Is it a gesture?

MB: Well, those two things. I think you've hit on them. The orchestra makes an incredibly intricate tapestry of sonority – it's very imaginative in that realm. From a gestural point of view, the debt to this almost Fauvist Russian folk tradition: it's of its time. Those are the things that Russian artists were juggling with. There are some sonorities, I have to confess, that remain in my ear as a source of great pleasure. It's not so much the famous E flat/E major chords stacked together in ['The Augurs of Spring'], but that incredibly insinuating alto flute solo against this little Theda Bara, walk-like-an-Egyptian dance . . .

AF: I know, with the cor anglais ['Ritual Action of the Ancestors'].

MB: I mean, it's so hokey, but it is haunting and it is part of my collection of earworms. It's one of the leading ones.

AF: You know, I think the bit I like best is the opening of the second part. That incredibly placid, waiting-for-all-hell-to-break-loose . . .

MB: Yeah, yeah, it's a beautiful moment, that anticipation. You know, when you say that, though, what you are doing, in a sense, is helping to reinvest a work that was designed to be pictorial and dance-like with a sense of anticipation and formal energy, and this is something which I also do naturally when I listen.

AF: Tell me about 'Opere della musica povera'. What is this?

MB: 'Musica povera' was an idea that I developed in response to being in Italy, just after the 'arte povera' movement was trending and dissolving again. This was in the 1970s. I was a resident at the American Academy in Rome, and I had friends who were artists in the Italian community and they took me to shows. And I was very taken both with the aesthetic energy of what they were doing with very ordinary materials as a kind of polemic against the high expenses of the art world as it was conceived in those days, but also by the politics of it. It reminded us of how art could be democratised and spread out among people if you returned to its most elemental characteristics. When I saw that, I wondered if there was some way music could do the same. I was not able to do it at the time, I have to say; it took me a long time to come to it, because you have to be able to relinquish, to some degree, the sumptuousness of certain sonic worlds – you have to go for the almost puritanical austerity that poverty enforces by its own rules. If you can imagine taking one's compositional tools away and saying, 'Well, what can I make with the simplest things?' – that's how it struck me.

I might say that somebody who I don't know has recently reviewed online somewhere these pieces of 'musica povera' of mine and pointed out, quite correctly I think, that despite my protestations that it is a 'musica povera' – and I do believe it is, in many ways – I tended to focus on the aspects of that idea which do not imply the destruction of the language of music itself. I do not actually write punk classical music, which this person was arguing was a part of 'arte povera'. And I agree. I mean, he has a picture of these cans of shit which Piero Manzoni put together – *merda d'artista*, artist's shit – clearly deigned to be a complete raspberry to art as a discipline, and moving towards the dissolution of all the métiers of art all together into a conceptual space. That is not what I do. I couldn't go that far, and I will concede it.

The guy who wrote the blog was very shrewd because he pointed out that Morton Feldman had said somewhere that music is already perfect and that's its problem. Once you start taking away skill and quality from music in the service of some other idea, you're not really talking about music any more. So my 'musica povera' doesn't do that, but it does ask the listener to go back to the elemental ABC of what actually matters when you listen. What can you assemble from simple things?

AF: Why did you want to do that?

MB: This was in the 1990s, for one thing. This was an era when people were starting to get wealthy again in the United States. Clinton's soft, middle-of-the-road, Democratic positioning, his bending over a little bit and pulling down his pants for the business community enabled a certain amount of energy to go towards people getting rich again; and people did get rich. As they did so and as the welfare state was somewhat deconstructed by Clinton, I think there was a danger of forgetting about a lot of parts of the US that were not in that state at all. I live most of my life in New Haven, Connecticut, which is a lovely town, but which is surrounded by towns that just didn't recover and are still struggling to recover from the decline of their former industrial strength. I wanted to remind people of that. And I also wanted to remind people again of the elemental things in music that could mean something and be important.

And, if you'll forgive me, I'll go one step further. There is in this work, I've come to see, a kind of hubris which says, 'Look, I can make this intricate, complicated, fancy thing out of almost nothing; I can do it with the tiniest of elements.' The commissions I received for doing these pieces were very small, on the whole – which also seemed appropriate – and I wanted to assemble these scraps to show, 'Yes, look what I can do with next to nothing.' You could get by on austerity, in other words. In the end, I suppose that works against itself. You know, if we're going to change austerity we don't want to get along with it – we want to make sure people have enough. I don't know how you do that in music, or in any art form. Auden said, 'Poetry makes nothing happen.' I'm not sure about that. I was trying to make *something* happen, at least in the awareness of the listener.

AF: And do you think you succeeded in making something happen?

MB: With all humility, I have to leave that to others to decide. I don't know.

AF: So how did you go about it? These pieces seem to have their starting points in a variety of references: Paul Klee, William Blake, Pinocchio. *The Bucket Rider* [1995] was inspired by a Kafka story; *Bird as Prophet* [1999] conflates Schumann and Charlie Parker. What, if anything, do these sources have in common?

MB: All the works begin on a single pitch or pitch horizon. They all move, in their interior sections, to another horizon a tritone away. It's the old 'axis of symmetry' that the tritone provides as a measure of distance and a contrast. All the works are characterised by pitch symmetries, and all are ABA formally. So while the exterior of the compositions might express very different affects or points of emotional departure, the interior, the skeleton and anatomy of the form, are in fact the same for all the 'Opere'. That is the architectural conceit of the cycle. From a referential point of view, all the works reflect some aspect of human – or, as in the case of *Pine Eyes* [Pinocchio], almost human – poverty and simplicity. It is up to attentive listeners to follow the literary, extra-musical signs I have left for them – or not – as they wish. There are, I hope, many ideas and sounds to attend to. As someone famously said, 'My father's house has many mansions . . .' I have tried to create many doors to my house. You are welcome to enter through any you wish.

AF: Does *Fantasia on a Theme by Willie Dixon* [2001] belong in the same company as your 'musica povera' pieces?

MB: Yes and no. Unlike the 'povera' works, the *Fantasia* is rather informal and occasionally humorous. It is often voluptuous in colour and quite virtuosic – as would be required for a 'rock'-based work that is also a small piano concerto. On the other hand, I have reduced the Willie Dixon tune ['Spoonful'] to only a fragment of the chorus – a simple minor third. That's pretty simple – so in that way it resembles the other 'Opere'.

AF: Do you think there's a danger for composers – for music – in too much refinement?

MB: You've stopped me cold. I think it depends upon your attitude towards pleasure. And I think there's a tendency on my part, and maybe in others too, to be a little suspicious of too much pleasure. I don't consider that an admirable characteristic of mine. I think Oscar Wilde may well have been right about this matter, and that the anxiety that people feel in the presence of pleasure and refinement actually restricts human abilities and capabilities and the freedom to be a human being. So I think there is no danger, but it still makes many of us nervous.

I've had arguments with people who seem constantly to worry that people will have too much of a good time when hearing a piece of music, and that this will be terrible. They think that if you like a piece, if it sounds beautiful, it can't be good: *ipso facto*, it cannot be good. There's too much refinement, it's too happy with its own means and ways, it provides too much pleasure, and the purpose of art is to be sermonic, to teach you something, to be didactic. Now, as Groucho Marx famously said, 'I resemble that remark.' I am a little bit like that myself, and it's not a part of me I'm so happy with.

AF: Can you name some examples of music from the past – in any style, in any genre – where you feel that the simplicity of materials or of technique has been a revivifying factor?

MB: I think that's a constant feature of music history; it happens all the time. From the most ornate and highly structured materials, there is almost always some sort of reaction that takes us back to very simple things. From the end of the Ars nova period [in the late fourteenth century] and those Chantilly Codex pieces of unbelievable complexity that can barely be performed today, you have over in the British Isles a master like Dunstaple and his followers writing parallel thirds and sixths, which seems to clear the air beautifully. I think this goes on and on, and I don't want to fetishise either development. I don't think it's impossible to make a beautiful piece out of very little, but I also don't think it's impossible to make a beautiful piece out of too much. There is no rule.

AF: Perhaps you'll refuse to see this as a clear-cut distinction, but throughout history there have been capital-C composers – composers who write things down – who have drawn on folk music, jazz, rock, hip-hop. Can you name any examples that have particularly impressed you?

MB: I think it's consistent and continuous. There's barely a composer who can find any distance from that position that you've just articulated. For instance, Haydn in the 'London' symphony [No 104 in D] borrows a Croatian folk song for the last movement and makes a lovely thing out of it, and there are many such borrowings from folk traditions or what are perceived to be folk traditions. Obviously, Bartók, a great hero of mine, does this. And I would urge people to go back and listen closely to another of my heroes, Janáček. Here's a guy who is so interested in the demotic that not only does he go out and collect folk songs, but he literally sits in cafes and listens to people talk, notates the rhythm and melody of their speech and uses these as generative features in his music.

Music has to come from somewhere. It can come from music, but it's often refreshed from other *kinds* of music and other places where music is made and, in the case of Janáček, from speech. I was listening again the other day to *Boris Godunov* by Musorgsky, and so much of it is Russian Orthodox church music or some variant of it, with folk tunes of various kinds beautifully rethought by this master. One of the legacies of modernism was to cast a dark shadow over that sort of activity, for many reasons which need not detain us, but I think it is inevitable that people will go outside their own genre to refresh it.

AF: What about brutality in music? It's something else which comes and goes, isn't it?

MB: It is, and I've been thinking about this too. It's stimulating sometimes to be hit over the head with a brick. There used to be a commercial in the United States where a woman comes up to a guy and slaps him in the face, and he says, 'Thanks. I needed that.' Actually, I think the Buddha does that in one of the tales – he slaps someone. Sometimes you get into a rut of behaviour that is self-defeating and reinforcing itself in its own repetition, and a jolt can be salutary.

One of my students when I was first teaching at Yale was the composer Michael Gordon. His music was so elemental and so brutal when he started out – and he can still do that when he wants to – that it really shocked me and set me thinking hard about some unexamined filigree in my music that perhaps needed a haircut or a close shave. Some of the great pleasures of my life in teaching have been encountering very strong young minds, whose direction is not mine but [who], by going the way they go, shine light on things that I wouldn't have seen otherwise. Michael's primitivism in the first piece that we worked on together, called *Thou Shalt!/Thou Shalt Not!* [1983] – as austere a piece as you could have; it's Old Testament-like in character – really stimulated me to rethink things, and it is part of why I ended up writing my Trio for violin, cello and piano of 1988, which really goes back to the basics again and leaves them very clear and transparent on the page.

AF: The four movements of the Trio seem to encapsulate many if not most of the elements of what would go on to become your 'musica povera'. There's a reference to a children's game, there are instructions such as *semplice* ('simply') and *ardente* ('ardently') and indeed *parlando* – 'speech-like' – which is an unusual term to encounter in instrumental music.

MB: Yes. The Trio is, among other things, an exhaustive demonstration of the various means of symmetry that I was working on from the time of my second string quartet of 1983–84. The Trio is almost medieval in its symmetrical obsessions. As I attempted to master a wide variety of symmetrical procedures, I noticed that such formally simple beauty could be found almost everywhere. Even the children's game Cat's Cradle, played with a single loop of string, was actually a way of creating a progressive set of elegant symmetrical patterns. Simplicity joined with sophisticated formal exigency! I was captivated – but also unsatisfied in the end. You will note the last movement of the Trio is marked *ardente, sperduto* or 'ardently, lost'! After all that precise ratiocination, it seemed to me something was missing. The work ends symmetrically but in confusion. Although I wrote several more very strict works like the Trio – *Pontoosuc* [1989], for orchestra, a third string quartet [1992] and some others – I became more and more interested in compositions with more obvious, non-formal attributes, like more pictorial and narrative 'Opere della musica povera'.

AF: The *parlando* instruction in the Trio strikes me as significant for another reason. Quite a few of your recent pieces involve actual speech. Not a narrator as in *Pine Eyes*, but speaking instrumentalists. The pianist Lisa Moore was, I imagine, the original inspiration for this, but there's also *A Message from the Emperor* [2010] for two speaking percussionists, and the chamber ensemble *My Twentieth Century* [2002], in which all the players speak. What's the attraction of the speaking voice? Do you regard the sound of speech as an element of 'poor music'?

MB: I am a great lover of poetry and literature generally. When I hear people speaking, or reading poetry aloud, I always hear that as music. My mother, who is now very old, has become a 'professional' storyteller. It is actually something she always did when I was growing up – telling stories of her old home in Russia, and other tales of coming to America. Now she makes a small income from it, although at ninety-two she can't get around like she used to. I think that speech and music are merely a continuum of expression in sound, both simple and complex in their own way. If you are, as I am, interested in the narrative possibilities of music, and music united with speech, it is natural to combine them. So now, at last, I am writing opera!

AF: In your home in New Haven, there's a picture of Brahms over your piano. He's one of my favourite composers, so I was pleased to see it. Now, there are many things I love about his music, but near the top of the list is the way he puts it together. He takes quite small things – three-note cells, whatever – and they seem inexhaustible in his hands, they proliferate endlessly. I wonder whether this is what appeals most to you, too, and whether there's a connection here with your 'musica povera'?

MB: Ah, Brahms! There are in fact very few works of mine that do not engage that master in one way or another. The foundational principle that beautiful, lyrical music should also be structurally elegant: that principle, that goal, I take from Brahms. Although Ligeti did not especially like Brahms – he once explained to me that, for him, Brahms was simply too 'healthy' – I have tried to marry Ligeti's freedom of affect and imagination with Brahms's formal musical architecture. I think many musical forms are simple and comprehensible to those listeners whose interest and listening skill lies there. To that extent, the 'Opere della musica povera' share a Brahmsian source.

5

The Sound of Skin

When I play the drums, they can, if I want, tell the story of a woman betrayed or a woman in love. They can tell the story of a train trip or a swim in the ocean.

Lindy Morrison,
drummer for the Go-Betweens

The Drift, Scott Walker's dark, disturbing album of 2006, is not his most harrowing work. Nonetheless, with vocals that seem perpetually distressed and occasionally verge on screaming, it makes tough demands on its listeners. If you think you can take it, try the track called 'Clara' and see if you can guess the provenance of that insistent dull slap. It sounds like a drum, but with absolutely no resonance. And really that is exactly what it is. Because what you are hearing is 'meat punching' – a member of Walker's band laying into a side of closely miked beef.

For at least five thousand years, drums have been made from animal skin stretched tightly across a frame or shell. Exceptions include the Vietnamese Dong Son drums, made of bronze, and various wooden drums – for example, African log drums. (Some would argue that, by definition, these are not drums, skin or membrane being the essential component of the family of instruments known as membranophones.) Even if, today, commercial drum heads are often plastic, they are still referred to as skins, while traditional drums continue to be made from animal hides: cow or calf, sheep, goat and donkey are the most commonly used, although there are even fish-skin drum heads. Scott Walker's meat puncher was simply cutting out the middle man.

It is hard to be precise about the drum in prehistory, because skin and wood decay faster than bone, say, from which various sorts of whistles were made. Images can show us drums – and there, indeed, they are, on cave walls in northern Africa and southern Europe. But it is impossible to know whether these are paintings of the first drums or simply the first paintings of drums. It seems likely that drum-like instruments were used long before the evolution of the more modern forms of drum. These would include hollow logs and planks of wood placed over a pit that could be jumped on, thus combining dance and musical accompaniment. These existed in a number of cultures, including the Solomon Islands, Indonesia and Malaysia. In New Guinea, India and Ethiopia there were earth drums, in which a hole dug into the ground created resonance when the opening was struck with the palm of the hand.

There is obviously something primal about the drum, something inescapably physical, and much of that is to do with the skin itself – skin that is either struck or stroked. But the fact that drums so often articulate pulse and rhythm is also part of their primal nature: if the drum is the most basic instrument, then pulse and rhythm are the most basic aspects of music. For we are all, even asleep, unwitting pulse makers – our hearts pump, we breathe in and out, and only death will stop us. We also are only slightly more aware rhythm makers. When we exercise or are excited, our pulses quicken, our hearts race, the beat becomes less regular, creating rhythmic variation (ideally, not too much rhythmic variation). When we skip or dance – or, for that matter, have sex – we also create rhythms with our bodies.

In beating out that rhythm, then, in sounding the pulse, the drum amplifies our lives and our *living*. In some cultures, drums have a familiar, domestic function – after all, the drum is one instrument that most people think they can play: who among us can walk past a drum without at least wanting to reach out to give it a tap? The Vietnamese rice drum is tuned with a ball of hot sticky rice attached to the centre of its skin (which expands, and so deepens in pitch), while the Irish bodhrán – in popular belief, at least – is tuned by liberally applying Guinness to the back of the skin prior to drying it before a peat fire.

Yet for all their familiarity, drums retain their mythical status. Drums precede important events. We hear a drum roll and are instantly expectant of an announcement, a circus act, a public execution. We sit in a darkened theatre and, before we hear a note, thrill to the sight of the elaborate drum kit raised up at the back of a rock band. In Japanese kumi-daiko (or group drumming) the gigantic, barrel-shaped ō-daiko – literally, 'big drum' – is a compelling, silent presence throughout the performance, as it waits to be struck. We know it won't be over till the fat drum sounds.

It is hard to know which came first, the mythical status or the ritual function, but it seems clear that for millennia drums have had both. The drum had potent spiritual significance in ancient Mesopotamia, where the frame drum was heard as early as 2700 BCE, and often used in spiritual contexts: the rectangular adapu frame drum might have had metal jingles and accompanied hymns and liturgies in religious ceremonies; the round mezu frame drum had a single head and it too was used for religious purposes, but also combined with other instruments for celebrations. The large su-ala drum, a couple of metres in diameter, was suspended from a frame positioned in front of temples from the third century BCE, although the drums themselves had already existed for three thousand years. And the lilissu, a large bronze kettledrum owned by the kalu-priest, who was in charge of temple chants, especially averting the deity's anger through music and lamentations, required a head made of the hide of a black bull free from blemishes. Killing the animal, obtaining the skin and skinning the drum were all done with ritual and ceremony.

In the Book of Psalms, which dates from around 1000 BCE, comes an injunction to 'Praise him with the timbrel and dance', a timbrel being a frame drum, the instrument of choice for many cultures when it came to worshipping their gods. It seems that in many Mediterranean, North African and Middle Eastern cultures, the playing of the frame drum was a woman's job. In the National Museum in Athens, there is a vase dating from the fifth century BCE that shows a woman playing a frame drum in an effort to help crops grow; a goddess is shown playing the tambourine and dancing in a Babylonian relief carving from the early twelfth century BCE (while the procession of gods before her carry weapons and play lutes); Sumerian figurines from 2000 BCE are of women playing frame drums; a baked clay plaque from the Diqdiqqa region near Ur shows a naked female figure holding a tambour. Similar images turn up in Egyptian carvings from 1300 BCE; indeed, the image was so common it appeared on Roman coins. In the Book of Exodus, we learn that 'Miriam the prophetess, the sister of Aaron, took a timbrel in her hand; and all the women went out after her with timbrels and with dances'.

The world is full of drums with religious uses. Tibetan Buddhists have small, double-headed prayer drums; the West African Yoruba and Hausa peoples use their sakara drums (clay pots with goat-skin heads) for prayer, and specifically to call worshippers to pray and feast during Ramadan; drums of various sorts have been used by shamans from North America to Africa to the Arctic Circle.

While drums may inspire us with their sonorities, their rhythms and their sheer volume, they are also precise enough to send signals and messages. So their other primary function is as instruments of war, and in this they are just as universal as in their devotional role. Military drummers can beat a tattoo or they can beat a retreat. And at funerals – at least, at the funerals of important political or military figures – the drums continue to beat, though draped in black to shroud their appearance and muffle their tone. In the famous march for 'flatt trumpets' that Henry

Purcell composed for the funeral of Queen Mary in Westminster Abbey in 1695, the muffled drums were probably kettle drums; since these would not have been allowed to be played in the Abbey itself, they must have been played en route, either strapped to a horse or carried on men's backs, during the coffin's journey from Whitehall.

Kettle drums – or timpani, to give them their common orchestral name – first came into the symphony orchestra together with trumpets. In eighteenth-century symphonies and concertos they always go together, their military origins plain enough. Even so, while the drums were a common sight and sound in the orchestra by the end of that century, they could still be worth remarking upon: the soft timpani roll at the beginning of Haydn's Symphony No 103 in E flat (1794–95) was apparently unusual enough to earn the work the nickname 'Drumroll symphony'.

In 1796, during the French Revolutionary Wars, the same composer wrote a Mass in C with a prominent part for timpani – now soft, now seemingly closer, and finally, in the 'Agnus Dei', heard on their own; there was considerable fear in Austria that year that the French would invade. On the score, in Haydn's own writing, are the words *Missa in tempore belli* ('Mass in a Time of War'), which the composer presumably intended as its title, but the Mass quickly gained the popular nickname of 'Paukenmesse', or 'Kettle Drum Mass'. When, a few years later, Haydn's old employer Nikolaus Esterházy commissioned Beethoven to compose a Mass, the composer produced his own Mass in C (1807) and borrowed the martial timpani from his teacher's 'Agnus Dei' for his 'Sanctus'.

In the new context, as Michelle Fillion has pointed out, the drums become part of God's army, not that of a foreign invader.

Both works demonstrate the early association of drums with warfare, and this is not a connection that ever completely goes away. Typically, the timpani have continued to present calls to arms – think of the pounding drums in the famous opening of Strauss's *Also sprach Zarathustra*, or in the brass fanfare that begins and ends Janáček's *Sinfonietta* – but composers also use them for their sonority, for their sheer drumminess.

When a modern symphony orchestra plays music from the last hundred years, there is often a battery of tuned and untuned percussion ranged across the back of the platform, but when we think of orchestral drums it is timpani that first come to mind. From the point of view of spectacle, nothing matches the timpanist sitting at the pinnacle of the orchestra, looking down on the other players and presiding over three, four or even five tuned drums. Occasionally, as in *The Rite of Spring*, there may even be two sets of timpani and two players. Like the ō-daiko, these timpani, their copper kettles glinting under the stage lighting, hold the promise of noise to come.

We tend to assume that sonority for its own sake, especially percussive sonority, is a twentieth-century development in music (the composer Varèse spoke of the 'liberation of noise', a step beyond Schoenberg's 'liberation of dissonance'). But consider a piece as well-known as Beethoven's *Pastoral* symphony, completed in 1808. In the fourth movement the timpani are providing sound effects – thunderclaps in a violent storm – but it is not the loud bangs that are so memorable or so realistic. Chopin, via George Sand, pointed out that in this movement Beethoven was not trying to convey the thunder so much as 'the shiver, the feeling of wonder, the terror of nature'. And yet, at the end of the movement, the timpani do a very convincing job of verisimilitude. As the storm passes, the kettle drums continue to provide a distant rumbling, and the moment is pictorial to the point of naturalism. Even as the first line of the chorale-like theme ushers in the shepherds' song of thanksgiving, the rumbling goes on, the timpani passing it to the cellos, which softly play their lowest note, and the double basses. Not only has Beethoven used the timpani independently of the trumpets, he has employed the drums' sonority as an intrinsic and almost equal part of his orchestration.

Berlioz's *Symphonie fantastique* (1830) is, to all intents and purposes, modelled on the Beethoven. Like the *Pastoral*, it is a programmatic symphony in five movements – the central one a bucolic fantasy – but even individual musical figures can be traced back to Beethoven. When it comes to the use of the timpani, though, Berlioz – the great Romantic colourist – goes much further than his hero. In particular, in the last three movements he calls for two timpani players and much retuning of the drums.

The most impressive use of the extra player and extra timpani is at the end of that third movement, the 'Scene in the Fields', where Berlioz has the drums play completely on their own. Taking his cue from Beethoven's distant rumbling thunder, Berlioz asks his players to execute simultaneous rolls across four drums, marked *ppp* (extremely quiet), making dramatic crescendos to *forte* and back again. It is a sound that is full of foreboding, a harbinger of the 'March to the Scaffold' and 'Witches' Sabbath' yet to come, but it is also a harbinger of the future of music, for it is impossible to escape the conclusion that in this passage, above all else, Berlioz is experimenting with percussive sonority. We have come a long way from the use of timpani to give point and emphasis to trumpet flourishes or to symbolise war. Berlioz's experimentation not only involves the production of hazy chords conjured from the simultaneous sounding of differently tuned drums, but also careful control of the tone of those drums. For the first time in musical history, Berlioz specifies in his score the precise nature of the sticks the two timpanists should be using at this point – mallets with soft heads made of sponge to muffle the sound of the individual strokes.

By now, the timpani were an established part of the symphony orchestra, although they were seldom employed as effectively as in *Symphonie fantastique*, or with the same degree of sophistication. Even today, nearly two hundred years after Berlioz featured the timpani as the rest of the orchestra fell silent, it is hard to escape the conclusion that these drums and percussion instruments in general remain exotic interlopers. But it is precisely their 'otherness' that allows drums to reinvigorate the sound of the orchestra, from Beethoven and Berlioz to Stravinsky and beyond. Simply, the drum is a less sophisticated instrument than a violin or a flute; it is more of the earth, more natural, more primitive.

* * *

While drums remain optional extras in an orchestra, in rock music it is the other way round. Drums are of the essence. A rock band without a drummer is really not a rock band. Providing a driving beat might always be the primary aim of a rock drummer, but sonority certainly plays a part. In fact, the sound of the drum is as important as it is in classical music, and often for the same reason. Just as composers in the concert hall use the sound of drums to conjure the earth, the violence of nature and the violence of humankind, the real and the raw, so do rock bands, and it is nearly always a matter of returning the music to something like its roots.

The immediate roots of rock and roll music lie in mid-1950s America, but there are deeper roots, too, in rhythm and blues and, more hazily, in Africa. It is that sometimes romanticised African connection that drums often seem to want to capture. Jazz musicians from Sidney Bechet and Duke Ellingtom to Benny Goodman had long evoked Africa in some of their numbers, always with renewed emphasis on the tom-toms. Bo Diddley was the first to try it in rock, the thumping sonority of his drummer's toms as powerful as Bo's own famous syncopated beat.

Another example of the raw power of tom-toms was Jerry Allison's nonstop paradiddle pattern in Buddy Holly's 'Peggy Sue' (1957), which delivers, on a smaller scale, a thrill similar to the continuous semiquavers of the timpani in 'Dance of the Earth'. Once again, it is the sonority of the drums as much as their relentless beating that stays in the mind.

The tom-toms are the heart of the rock drummer's kit. Most kits have at least one or two toms, including a floor tom. The sound of these drums has been very influential in rock music, even if it goes unnoticed by many listeners, eclipsed, perhaps inevitably, by the singers and guitarists who are the stars of rock. If ever a drummer was eclipsed in this manner, it was the much misunderstood Ringo Starr, but in his work with the Beatles he was actually something of a pioneer, particularly in the area of the tom-tom. Ringo tuned his tom-toms down, producing not only a deeper tone but also a less reverberant sound because of the slackened heads. He also sat higher behind his kit than most drummers so that gravity aided his heavy and reliable back-beat. He made great use of the floor tom, too – in film clips you can see him reaching down to hit it from his high stool. He maintained that his left-handedness added to the unconventionality of his technique, but what is certain is that his distinctive manner, in turn, helped create the Beatles' sound.

Direct African influences came into pop even before 'world music' had been invented, courtesy of field recordings. An early example, actually by a South African musician, was John Kongos's looped recordings of tribal drumming, complete with hortatory vocalisations and other field-recording ambience on his 1971 hits 'He's Gonna Step on You Again' and 'Tokoloshe Man'. To the recorded drumming Kongos added tom-toms in the former, congas in the latter, and four decades later his four sons, in their band named simply Kongos, continued to draw inspiration from African drumming. John Kongos never revealed the source of the recording on his tape loop, but Kongos plays at least some of its percussion-heavy songs in the style of the Royal Drummers of Burundi. This centuries-old traditional style, which involves a degree of what one can only call swing (somewhere between a slightly lazy dotted rhythm and a triplet beat), can be clearly heard on songs such as 'I'm Only Joking' from Kongos's first album, *Lunatic* (2012).

A more famous example of the use of field recordings is the recording of the Burundi drummers heard on Joni Mitchell's album *The Hissing of Summer Lawns* (1975). It comes on a song called 'The Jungle Line', that distinctive swinging beat with its unpredictable accents providing the backing rhythm of the entire song, while a distorted Moog synthesiser adds a repeating riff and Mitchell sings of the French post-impressionist painter Henri 'Le Douanier' Rousseau. Rousseau's best-known works are his jungle scenes, often featuring tigers or lions, the latter occasionally lunching on gazelles. During his lifetime, it was rumoured that Rousseau's jungles were painted on location, but in fact he never left France. The animals were stuffed or based on illustrations in books, and the plants were painted in glasshouses in Paris's botanical gardens. 'The Jungle Line' is a very good song with a very striking sound; somehow, a synthesised riff added to purloined African drumming – misattributed on the original LP sleeve – seems right for Rousseau.

It was around the time of Mitchell's album that synthesised drums began to be heard. It is strange to think that this ubiquitous sound of 1980s pop might once have been considered part of experimental music's 'cutting edge', but some of the earliest uses of the technology were by bands such as 'krautrockers' Can on side four of their influential double album *Tago Mago* (1971), and Pink Floyd in their music for Barbet Schroeder's film *La Vallée*

(1972), reworked on their album *Obscured by Clouds* (1972). It took the perfection of the programmable drum machine in the mid-1970s, coinciding with the heyday of disco music, for the technology suddenly to flourish.

But the machine fooled no one – and neither was it meant to. In fact, one of the things the drum machine achieved was a whole new respect for the sound of a real drum. As though to emphasise the point, some stadium rock bands added a second drummer. If nothing else, it provided a certain visual reassurance, but really it served to underline the importance of the drum and the sound of the drum. Rock music is best returned to its roots by increasing the level and quality of the drumming. The less synthesised the percussion, and the more it sounds like wood hitting skin, the more authentic it is.

* * *

Composers began writing for ensembles of percussion instruments alone in the 1930s. The instrumentation of Stravinsky's *Les noces* and Antheil's *Ballet mécanique* had surely paved the way, but each of those scores is as famous for its multiple pianos as for its mass of percussion. Varèse's *Ionisation* (1933) was the first piece for percussion alone – at least, the first to become widely known – and while among the list of thirty-four instruments there was a piano in this work, too, it was used sparingly and only at the end of piece, to produce tone clusters in its lower range, where it sounded like a big gong. The natural temptation in percussion pieces is to use as many colours and as much gear as possible, but as early as 1939

John Cage realised that a special sort of intensity might be achieved by limiting the instruments to a single type. *Construction in Metal* (later *First Construction in Metal*) concentrated on gongs and cymbals, anvils and brake drums; there's a piano in this piece, too, but its timbre is changed with metal rods laid on the (after all, metal) strings.

The two composers who really put the sound of skin at the forefront of their percussion music in large-scale works were Steve Reich and Iannis Xenakis, though their approaches were completely different. In calling his piece *Drumming* (1970–71), Reich was drawing attention to the West African drumming tradition that, to some extent, lay behind his music. It was not that he borrowed specific techniques from the music he heard and saw performed on a visit to Ghana just before beginning work on his piece – by 1970 he had already used the phasing technique in *Drumming* plenty of times before, and he said that the visit confirmed him in his musical direction, rather than changing it – but there was something about the appearance of this work that suggested African drummers joining in a performance, dropping out, taking a rest and then coming back to it.

For Reich, however, the drums in *Drumming* were the beginning of something else. The four sets of tuned bongos are heard on their own only in Part One of the piece, before the music moves on to marimbas and glockenspiels, and indeed to singing voices and a piccolo in the later parts, finally bringing everything together in Part Four. It is as though the drums represent something basic from which melody might start to emerge.

In his sextet *Pléïades* (1978), Xenakis reversed this procedure. Taking its title from the constellation and the Greek myth for which it is named, as well as the more literal meaning of 'many', *Pléïades* is as much about the visceral experience of sound as it is about rhythm. Like Reich's *Drumming*, it is in four parts, each with a different instrumentation, but unlike in *Drumming*, the performers can choose the order of the sections. In 'Mélange' all the instruments are heard, in 'Claviers' just keyboard percussion (vibraphones, marimbas and so on), in 'Métaux' the players perform exclusively on 'sixxens', metal plates tuned microtonally and designed specially for this piece by the composer, and in 'Peaux' ('Skins') it is drums alone.

One imagines that Xenakis originally expected that players would choose to end the work with 'Mélange', the part that brings all the instruments together. But after numerous performances by groups across the world – for *Pléïades* is a classic – a clear preference emerged to finish with the drums on their own. So where Reich's piece progresses from the basic sound of bongos, Xenakis's moves from the ringing pitches of tuned instruments towards the primitive thump of beaten skin. The music of 'Peaux' is loud, rhythmic and insistent, and it never fails to thrill.

6

Song of the Earth

AN INTERVIEW WITH KARIN REHNQVIST

Karin Rehnqvist (born in Stockholm in 1957) is a hugely distinctive composer, nearly all of her music related in one way or another to the vocal practice of kulning. *These are piercingly loud herding calls, and they feature in most of Rehnqvist's vocal music, some of her choral works and even some of her purely instrumental pieces. The interview took place, via Skype, in May 2014, with later editing and some supplementary questions dealt with by email.*

ANDREW FORD: What is a herding call?

KARIN REHNQVIST: It is a special way of using the voice. It was used for calling for cows and goats by young girls, often out on their own in the countryside or in the mountains. They'd use this very special vocal technique, very different compared to classical singing. You raise the larynx and you try to throw the sound straight ahead. And it could be heard for kilometres, actually. It was used for cattle but also to communicate to other people over long distances.

AF: So did it develop the way that it did because of its ability to carry?

KR: Yes. It's also mostly very high in register, but it differs in different areas in Sweden. Sometimes it's just chest voice and sometimes it's very high up. But it was always from the need to be very loud.

AF: Did you hear these calls as a child? Have they always been part of your experience?

KR: No, not at all. I'm from the south of Sweden, a small city in Småland, and I didn't hear it there. And I didn't hear folk music at all; though it was there, actually, I didn't meet it. I was singing in the church choir. I heard folk music first when I came to Stockholm, at the age of twenty, when I started my studies at the Royal College of Music. I just felt immediately that it was my music, so to speak, so I started to play it and started to sing it. And then *kulning* – these special herding calls – the first time I heard that was in my own piece, *Davids nimm* [1983]. This piece, based on a polska played backwards, is for three female voices, and it's the piece where I found my style. One of the singers used this technique. In one part of the piece she had to go from very low pitches to very high pitches, and on the high pitches she produced this very piercing sound. So I wondered, What is this? Okay: it's *kulning*! Then, later, I wrote *Puksånger-lockrop* [1989], where the main idea was to use this technique.

AF: So you were drawn to the sound? It wasn't the historic associations, it wasn't the folkloric origins – it was simply the noise it made that appealed to you?

KR: Yes, it was actually the sound. I just loved it. It had nothing to do with other associations. But then I am also very interested in history and in forms of expression that have remained with us, like the call and the prayer and the incantation and so on. I'm very interested, in fact, in communication, which this is about. But the first thing was only the sound – and also the melodies used in the herding calls.

AF: So what did you hear in the calls that you didn't hear in the vocal music of your classical training? Was there something else? Something extra? Something different?

KR: Yes, it's very powerful. And, I mean, being a young girl [laughs] and hearing this very, very powerful sound that is not at all trying to be sweet and nice and beautiful . . . that appealed to me a lot.

AF: I'm sure it would have been explained to you very quickly that this was an ancient sound. But did you also hear something modern in it?

KR: Absolutely. It's very modern, I think. It's raw and powerful, and very focused. And also it has this *non vibrato* sound that I like very much. Also I realised it might be possible to have two voices using this technique at the same time, and very close to one another. That had never been done before. That was something really different.

AF: How did you set about using this sound? Did you simply take the technique or did you also take genuine herding calls?

KR: I've done both, but I started by just using the technique because I wanted to work with these singers – these folk singers, Lena Willemark and Susanne Rosenberg. We were studying together at the Royal College of Music in Stockholm. They were able to read scores, which not all folk musicians are. So I really wanted to work with them. We were very close and we are still very close; they are very good friends and we have the same outlook on life. So *Puksånger-lockrop* also came out of who these singers were and what we had experienced together. So they were really very important.

And I used also timpani – *Timpanum Songs–Herding Calls* is the English title of *Puksånger-lockrop* – because I wanted to use in the piece what we human beings had from the beginning: we had our voices and also something we could beat on. So that's why it became a piece for percussion and voices. But, typical me, it was a very complicated percussion instrument that I chose, the timpanum. It's not just a piece of wood or something. It's a technically very complicated instrument.

AF: So how does the piece work?

KR: It starts actually with a kind of fanfare, but instead of trumpets, it's voices. This is something I realised only afterwards. From this very, very loud and very high beginning, immediately you go as low as possible with the voices. It's a piece which really uses the voices in extreme registers, which is possible for these singers because they also have very low chest voices. Also there are always two sorts of material in a dialogue, so to speak. The first is a folk song, [sings] 'Der for två vita duvor' ['Two white doves went to the vault of heaven'] – just sections of it – and then in between I put a text from a Mexican shaman woman, [sings] 'Jag börja i vattnets djup . . .' ['I begin in the depths of the water'] – very low!

And what happens is that from this very high start to this very low register, you expect that the music will rise again because it is so low. But you should always do the opposite, I think! In a composition you can go with expectations or against them. And so from this low register, it goes further and further down – *very* low – until suddenly there is a big jump up two octaves or something, actually on the word 'djup' – 'depth'. I thought, afterwards, that when you are standing very high, you can look down and see the depth . . .

The piece is in five sections, and they also use other sounds from herding calls – like [grunting] 'Uh! Uh, uh!' – a rough sound. And in one section they sing, also from a Swedish folk song, [sings] 'Det växte upp en lilja i gröndalen . . .' ['A lily grew in the green valley'], like this, and it's very delicate, lots of small words and very, very soft, and then suddenly: 'Uh! Uh, uh!' It's like, you know, you are very civilised and very nice all the time, and suddenly there's a wild animal coming out from inside you! That's my thought about it, afterwards. And then the last section uses this *kulning* technique, and it sounds like a traditional herding call, but it's not – I wrote it myself. So I'm really mixing things, using parts of old songs, but in the way I want.

AF: Did you have any qualms about doing that? Did it ever occur to you that maybe you shouldn't write your own herding calls, that there was something sacrosanct about these folk songs and techniques?

KR: Often when you get an idea, it's a very clear moment and you remember it. And I remember, while I was driving the car, getting this idea for the 'Uh!' just coming into the song suddenly, and I thought, Whoops, that's dangerous! I shouldn't do that. But on the other hand, there's something about it that needs to be said when you have that feeling. Also, I know so much about Swedish folk music. I've learnt a lot from my friends, so I just feel very comfortable with it. I'm not picking just anything. I always use the seed – do you say that? 'frö'? – and enlarge it, in a way. I mean, I feel related to Bartók in some way, in this regard. He also used folk music from great knowledge. And Swedish folk music is not about nice chords in a romantic way, but it's about melodies and lines and drones, and the lines are often very close together – heterophonic and so on – and that's also the way I've used it.

AF: Let's talk about one or two of your other pieces before moving on to something more general. I'm not even sure how to pronounce this title: *Quem chama?* [2008].

KR: Actually, I'm not sure of it myself, because it's Portuguese! Because it was done for Casa da Música in Porto. In English, it's 'Who's That Calling?'.

AF: Well, the word 'calling' keeps appearing in your titles, in what you write about music and sometimes in the texts that you set, but in this particular case, the calling was given quite a dramatic shape.

KR: Yes. Here I'm using traditional herding calls, and I'm also mixing them with instruments – trumpets and trombones at the beginning. This piece is a bit about spacing, because the first singer and two trumpets are in the concert hall, up in the choir gallery straight ahead, and then at the back of the hall is the other singer and two trombones, so you can really hear the sound, how it goes through the hall. And then, on the stage, there is an ensemble of nine instruments. And there is a section which is kind of improvisational, where the singers use herding calls in another way: they say, [high-pitched, then falling] 'Kit, kit, kit, kit, kit – come, we have nice grass here!' And they name all the cows and all the goats. And I have written into the score that the instruments should answer – like, *be* the animals – which they found very funny, and they really liked, too.

AF: Does the shape of this piece change depending upon the kind of space in which it's performed?

KR: A bit, yes. Casa da Música is a very long hall – it's quite a distance from front to back. And now the piece has been performed in the Royal Festival Hall in London, and instead of having the singer with the trombones at the back, they were up on the balcony, quite high, which was also very nice, I think.

AF: *Ropade någon?* ['Was Someone Calling?', 2006] is another piece that has an element of space and indeed drama. Your website actually describes it as a 'happening'.

KR: Yes. It was made for the market place in Stockholm – Hötorget – which is outside the Stockholm Concert Hall. It used the balconies on the outside of the building – two folk singers and three brass instruments, each on their own balcony. I was down below, trying to conduct a bit, and they were singing and playing. And a lot of friends were out in the market place with bells and triangles and different percussion instruments. And then I had spoken to the hawkers in the market, saying that when they hear these bells they should start calling out whatever they call every day. So they were calling, 'Half price, half price! . . . Buy today, pay tomorrow!' And it really, really worked. There were a lot of people on the steps outside the concert hall, and it was a sunny day. Very good indeed.

And someone told me also, which was interesting, that if you were standing near where I was conducting, then you heard the brass instruments very well and also the singers, but if you were standing on the other side of the square, you heard the singing voices much more. So that tells you something about the *kulning* technique – that you hear it far away. And then suddenly an ambulance came by [impersonates an ambulance siren], and that fitted really well!

AF: And this piece can be repeated?

KR: Absolutely. In fact, *Quem chama?* is based on this piece. It uses some of the same material for singers, though the ensemble sections are new and the piece as a whole is bigger.

AF: It makes a nice connection with those pieces from the Renaissance – you know, *Les cris de Paris* and *The Cries of London* – that involved the calls of street vendors.

KR: Yes, absolutely. Yeah. And I got a review in the daily newspaper that said you expected the cars to come out of the car park, like cows, in response to the calls! Because *kulning* is really something you react to.

AF: The other piece I particularly want to ask you about is *Rädda mig ur dyn* ['Rescue Me from the Mire', 1994]. Listening to the piece, it is hard in places to know if you are hearing a voice or a saxophone. They swap roles and blend alarmingly at times.

KR: Yes. I'm very, very interested in this: how do instruments and voices connect, and where are the points of connection in sound, in timbre? And this is for saxophone and *kulning*, which are very close to each other in timbre. This piece is actually like a *bouillon* of my music: it's very short, and it's as high as possible, as low as possible, as loud as possible and as soft as possible – big extremes all the time. And it's also based on a Swedish folk hymn that is sung in church – every village has its own hymns – and I just picked one small phrase. I used a couple of musical phrases from the hymn and a line from the Bible – 'Deliver me out of the mire' [from Psalm 69], only in Swedish. And the idea for the piece also came from the fact that, in Swedish, 'mire' is 'dy', which is also one of the syllables used for *kulning*. So it's: 'Rädda mig ur [suddenly in a high-pitched *kulning* voice] *DYN!*'

AF: You said that *kulning* is very close to the sound of the saxophone; it's also very close to the clarinet. And you've had a fruitful relationship with the clarinettist Martin Fröst.

KR: Yes.

AF: Is it fair to say that almost everything you compose now can be traced back to *kulning*?

KR: Almost everything. It's always there in some way. I've done a piece called *Raven Chant* [2007/2012], where I tried to get the *kulning* sound by mixing the trumpet and saxophone in a special way.

I've used it in orchestral music. And also with children's voices! They are good at *kulning* because they don't try to do anything else – they just sing. It's hard to do it if you are classically trained, because in classical music the larynx should be down low and in *kulning* it's high. But I have one piece, *In Heaven's Hall* [1998], for children's choir, including four singers who do *kulning*, and it's sung a lot – all over the world. There is also a version for mixed choir. Choirs started making their own versions, so I thought it was better to do one myself.

AF: Are you still interested in the classically trained voice?

KR: Absolutely. At the moment I am writing an opera. Also I've composed a lot for choirs and for solo classical singers. Using folk singers has its good things and its limitations, and it's the same with classical singers. No, I just like the voice, and I like to mix it with instruments and orchestras very much. But this folk-music way of singing is close to my heart.

AF: I have the feeling that writing for children tends to stigmatise the composer. It's not regarded as serious work. Benjamin Britten strikes me as unique, in that here is an indisputably major composer, and among his very finest works are pieces for children to perform. I can't think of another composer of whom that could be said. Or maybe it's you! Anyway, would you tell me more about writing for children's voices? *Ljus av ljus* ['Light of Light', 2003], for instance.

KR: I have written a lot for children's voices. I love the sound and, as often for composers, it comes from a fruitful collaboration with a choir and its conductor – Adolf Fredrik Girls Choir, and Bo Johansson, who started the choir and was their leader for thirty-eight years. To compose serious pieces for children – as artistically serious as for professional musicians – which challenge the singers in a good way, has been important to me. Children are capable of so much if you don't tell them this is difficult!

Ljus av ljus was a commission for children's choir and symphony orchestra for the Présences-Festival in Paris. My starting point is often an idea about timbre, and here I imagined a very shimmering and intense timbre. I wanted the sound of choir and trumpet to blend so as to emphasise the power of children, and the shimmering would come out of the strings' tremolo in a high register. It is important to give the choir 'acoustical room' by using orchestration and chords chosen to enlarge the sound of the voices. Then the singers don't have to struggle to be heard. In the third movement the room gets wider, when the trombones start to play from the surrounding balconies.

AF: Do you think there's a connection between your use of folk music in general and your attraction to ancient texts? Of course I know you work with modern poets as well, but among your pieces there are quite a lot of responses to Icelandic texts and Old Norse and old Finnish proverbs . . . and the Bible, of course, in one way or another. And Shakespeare is there . . . Is this part of a connection that you are seeking to make with the past?

KR: It is just another love, that of old texts. I love old ways of expression, as well as modern – although the Romantic I am not that fond of. How the text sounds is as important as the semantic meaning. It is also important to chose texts which are easy to speak out loud, not only to read silently. That is why I am very fond of the poems from old hymns – for instance, from the Swedish hymnal, which I grew up singing in the church choir as a child. They often use short words with important meaning. I try to use the more universal verses, which could relate to human beings in general, and are not so 'confessional'.

AF: And the Haya language – how did you find your way to that? Since, I assume, you don't speak the language at all, did this in some way free you as a composer? Or did it bring greater responsibilities?

KR: Actually, the language used in the choral piece *Haya!* [2009] is one I invented myself. I couldn't find any text I wanted to use, so I composed the piece, knowing only the first word: 'Haya!' After that, I fitted made-up words to it. I wanted the sound of lots of consonants. It was not that easy to get a language which didn't sound like a real language. I don't know if I succeeded. I called the language Hayan because of that first word. I didn't realise there actually *was* a Hayan language! I ought to have known, since I was actually in Tanzania in the area where the Haya people live!

AF: One of your most recent pieces – *All Those Strings!* [2014] – is for the Kronos Quartet plus kantele, the Finnish zither. A new old sound for you! Tell me about this piece.

KR: The sound of the kantele is really fascinating. It is very fragile and penetrating at the same time, sounding like something between harp and harpsichord. I wanted the piece to be a real interaction between the quartet and the kantele. Where could the timbres of the instruments meet? How could they blend? That made me use a lot of extended techniques for the strings.

I really tried out a lot of things for the strings, as well as the kantele, which I worked out in close collaboration with Ritva Koistinen, the player. My first idea was an ostinato, though in many variations, played by the second violin, viola and cello, *sul tasto* [bowing over the fingerboard] and very soft. It made me think of a cold winter's night. The kantele and first violin play obligato lines above, like stars and like the Northern Lights, with glissandi and harmonics. The mix of timbres produced something special, I think.

One of the movements is a very sweet melody, played first by the kantele, then involving the cello. The violins and viola play tremolo. Since playing the kantele is as much about dampening strings that should not ring as [it is about] plucking, this movement is also about sound and silence in dialogue. The piece ends as it begins, with falling, the kantele playing a scale from the middle register to the very bottom, where the kantele has thick strings which sound wonderful.

7

Crying Out Loud

I too am not a bit tamed – I too am untranslatable;
I sound my barbaric yawp over the roofs of the world.
'Song of Myself', *Leaves of Grass*, Walt Whitman

The final track on the Beatles' first LP contains the sound of a man shredding his vocal cords for our listening pleasure. 'Twist and Shout' had first been a hit for the Isley Brothers in 1962, and by the time the Beatles entered the Abbey Road studios to record *Please Please Me* in February 1963, it was already a John Lennon party piece. That's how the producer George Martin knew to save the song till the end of the session.

In the early 1960s, a pop album – particularly a first album – could be recorded, as it were, live, so the fourteen tracks of *Please Please Me* were done in a bit under ten hours. Because Lennon habitually wrecked his voice singing 'Twist and Shout', and in fact had a cold on the day of the recording, Martin gambled that the final fifteen minutes of the session would be sufficient to commit the song to tape. As it turned out, it was longer than required. A second take was attempted but, in Martin's words, 'John's voice had gone'.

So there it is: a moment in history, an entirely live, two-and-a-half minute performance, as exciting today as it was in 1963. And part of the excitement, no doubt, is the fact that we can hear that Lennon's voice is on the verge of packing in. This is not just extreme singing, not just rock and roll shouting, it is something more. The urgency in the voice comes, one might say, from life, from living. All singing is to some degree artifice, but Lennon's raw, primitive singing of 'Twist and Shout' approaches reality. We recognise, in the actual timbre of the voice, the sound of desperate pleading, and far from finding it ugly or distressing, we thrill to it.

Rock music, like the blues before it, aestheticised pain, and many of the best rock singers learnt to synthesise the sounds of suffering with considerable accuracy. Much of the time, the grit in the voice was intended to simulate sexual desire or ecstasy, the principal subjects of pop songs since the time of the troubadours. In soul music there was an indirect connection to religious ecstasy, the shouting and screaming of a Ray Charles or an Aretha Franklin almost interchangeable with that of a Southern preacher.

One of the most interesting intersections of sexuality and spirituality in pop music was found in the voice of Van Morrison, whose singing of lyrics was always on the verge of disintegrating into wordless grunting and growling. In a sense, this is the subject of his song 'Listen to the Lion' (1972). In a live performance of the song included on the album *It's Too Late to Stop Now* (1974), Morrison extends the line 'Listen to the lion inside of me', repeating the final words over and over, turning it into a nonsense mantra: 'side o' me side o' me side o' me side o' me . . .' This gradually gives way, as so often with Morrison, to wordless singing that, in this case, swings back and forth between controlled scatting and actual roaring. There are places in which he is not singing at all any more. Instead, we hear something akin to his vocal essence.

* * *

When it comes to vocal artifice, of course, the Western classically trained voice has few rivals, and here there is no attempt at all to emulate real life. The classical voice is a lovely but almost wholly unnatural thing, and over the centuries has moved only further from reality. Composers, from Monteverdi to our own day, have tried to inject something grittier, more naturalistic, even something uglier into their vocal lines, hoping to bring their music closer to reality, but singers have tended to resent and resist these attempts, and have sometimes found ways around it: we may read letters by Mozart and Rossini complaining about their singers and their tendency simply to show off and add ornamentation willy-nilly. Wagner was insistent that his music–dramas should be performed by singing actors, rather than singers, the acting in the voice as much as the body; Schoenberg's embrace of *Sprechstimme* – literally, 'speech voice' – in a number of works, most famously *Pierrot lunaire*, blurs the distinction between speaking and singing, and forces classical singers to abandon the smooth, *legato* lines they love to employ. Very occasionally, of course, a singer comes along who is prepared to abandon beauty of tone for dramatic verisimilitude; the American soprano Maria Callas was one such. But she was rare and we remember her for it.

Most singing voices involve a degree of training, albeit perhaps self-training, but in very few cultures is beauty of tone an end in its own right. The voice is there to sing songs, to tell stories in music, and the more the voice can convey the meaning of the words and the range of emotions in the story, the better the singer. This seems to be true throughout Africa, Asia and Aboriginal Australia. It is also true in the folkloric traditions of Europe.

One of the most vivid examples of this is Karelian lamenting. There are various sorts of lament in the world. There are, for example, plenty of composed laments that are, to all intents and purposes, simply sad songs about death. Then there are now largely extinct vocal traditions, such as keening, prevalent in Ireland and parts of Scotland until at least the eighteenth century. Keening – literally 'crying' – seems to have been entirely improvised, but we cannot be sure how it sounded. Perhaps the high-pitched ululation of Arab women comes close. The simultaneous wailing and tongue trilling that characterises this vocal style in the Arab world and parts of Africa is associated (because of the nightly news) with mourning, but equally it can be an expression of joy. It is the same with Karelian lamenting.

Unlike Celtic keening and Arab/African ululation, the laments of Karelia, Ingria and south-eastern Finland were not really improvised. The structural templates and much of the musical and verbal content of these laments are ancient and fixed, and so closer to folk song. Even so, the individual singer was able to personalise the material, as much as anything through her ability to harness her own grief.

The women who sang these laments had a special place in their society. Though hardly professionals in any sense we would recognise, they could be called upon to bring their laments to funerals and weddings, leading expressions of communal grief; the grief at weddings was associated most often with a daughter leaving the family home, and specifically her mother – a celebratory grief, you might say. The lamenting tradition had effectively died out by the middle of the twentieth century, but we have recordings, and from them we can gauge just how affecting these performances were, a heady, tragic mix of method acting, psychodrama and something like shamanism.

In Ingria in 1914, Harkina Martintytär sings a dirge over her mother's grave in which she imagines digging up her body and wiping the sand from her; in Vuokkiniemi in 1952, Domna Huovinen addresses her dead husband and implores those relatives who have gone on before to welcome him with lighted candles; at Kiuruvesi in 1966, Pelagea Kuljukka laments finding herself a refugee from the Finnish region of Lake Ladoga following the Soviet invasion in the Winter War of 1939–40.

In most of these laments, the singer begins tentatively, exploring the song and the heavy sentiments behind it in a manner that brings to mind a classical Indian musician mapping out a raga in the introductory *alap*. The *alap* is usually expansive and deliberate, while the start of the lament is merely diffident, but in each there is the same sense of the music being constructed by the performer before our very ears. The lamenting singer punctuates her song with moans, wails or sobs, in the process robbing it of a strict metre. But as she gets further into her performance, seemingly growing in confidence, she generally hits what, in another context, one might call a groove, the song's metre stabilising as the performance becomes rhythmically stricter (the raga comparison holds). What happens next is very interesting: the sob takes on a new role as a kind of insistent and almost percussive refrain, and the singer's grief becomes fully part of the musical fabric.

Thinking of Stravinsky's *Les noces* and Bartók's *Three Village Scenes* in the context of these recordings of Karelian laments is instructive. *Les noces* begins with a scene in which a bride laments her situation while her mother braids her hair; there are many braiding laments in the Karelian tradition. In the first of the *Village Scenes*, a bride goes off to her husband's village while her family and friends squeal with a high-pitched 'Hi-ji-ji-ji-ji-ji-ji-ji!' – very close to ululation. It is significant that these works – *Les noces*, a milestone of early modernism, and *Village Scenes*, a homage to *Les noces* – should have drawn so directly on traditional singing to create modern music; it is interesting, too, that some of this inspiration came, at least indirectly, from sounds of human distress.

Next to the work of Yoko Ono and Diamanda Galás, of course, Stravinsky's and Bartók's pieces sound quite jolly. At the more experimental end of rock music, human distress has long been a recurrent part of the singer's arsenal of sounds, and the Japanese Ono, whose work already embraced the visual arts, filmmaking, poetry and performance art, made much use of extreme vocals on her debut solo album, *Yoko Ono/Plastic Ono Band* (1970), drawing, in particular, on sounds inspired by the primal therapy she and her husband, John Lennon, had undertaken.

The first track, 'Why', begins with Lennon's guitar screaming, before Ono's voice enters in vivid imitation; perhaps the guitar simply anticipates the vocals. In 'AOS', Ornette Coleman's trumpet shadows Ono as she sings/wails at first tenderly, then seductively, then with alarming violence, and finally gently petering out; in 'Don't Worry, Kyoko (Mummy's Only Looking for Her Hand in the Snow)', which is not on the album but was recorded at the same time, Ono's long-drawn-out and actually rather virtuosic wails are extended and embellished by Eric Clapton's guitar. Perhaps the stand-out track from the album, however, is 'Paper Shoes', in which her wailing is carried along on top of rich, relentless drumming by Ringo Starr: a double layer of primitive sound, which is fused by Lennon's guitar into something rather less primitive.

Ono was an acknowledged influence on Galás, an American performance artist, composer and a singer with five octaves at her disposal, who has tended to specialise in the kind of subjects that require the voice to be used *in extremis*, including mental illness. The death of her brother in 1986 from an AIDS-related illness reinforced her involvement with AIDS activism, but she had already begun her operatic trilogy, *The Mask of the Red Death* (1986–89), following it up with *Plague Mass* (1991), recorded live at the Cathedral of St John the Divine in New York.

Galás's vocal style ranged from low, guttural noises to high-pitched screaming, her stamina in performance as impressive as her range. Clearly she was in complete control of her work, but a listener could be forgiven for thinking – and was, perhaps, expected to believe – that the screaming was 'for real'. A similar confusion arises with the later work of Scott Walker, particularly the trilogy of albums *Tilt* (1995), *The Drift* (2006) and *Bish Bosch* (2012), in which the vocals are frequently matched or enhanced by electronics. Writing in the *Guardian* about the final instalment, Alexis Petridis remarked that at the beginning of the album, 'drums . . . aren't so much being pounded as punished, overlaid with a kind of electronic shriek. And this is one of the more approachable moments on *Bish Bosch*.'

* * *

Galás probably belongs more to the world of high art than rock, and arguably so does Walker's trilogy, but screaming and shouting has been part of rock and roll since it was invented. In 1976, at the height of the British punk movement, the Slits was an all-female band (most of the time), formed by the Spanish drummer Palmolive (Paloma Romero) and fourteen-year-old German vocalist Ari Up (Ariane Forster), later joined by Tessa Pollitt and Viv Albertine on bass and guitar.

Combining the raw energy of punk with a more political outlook, not least by virtue of their name, the Slits were also strikingly original musically, especially at first. Ari Up's high-spirited *Sprechstimme* on 'In the Beginning There Was Rhythm' is bold and brilliant and really unlike much else that had gone before it, though it paved the way for a lot that came after. When the jazz trumpeter Don Cherry toured with the Slits in 1979, he brought along his fifteen-year-old Swedish-born step-daughter, Neneh.

Later the same year, she was singing with the band. The following year, the thirteen-year-old Annabella Lwin, the daughter of a Burmese father and a Liverpudlian mother, joined the band Bow Wow Wow as its vocalist.

What all three singers had in common (apart from being underage and of cosmopolitan parentage) was a high-energy girlish confidence that seemed wholly unaffected by technique or (as you might expect) experience. Of course, that didn't last, and ten years later Neneh Cherry's hit album *Raw Like Sushi* (1989) was the work of a twenty-five-year-old artist who had both technique and experience, but, *pace* the album's title, could have done with a little more rawness.

The riot grrrl movement that developed in 1991 from the underground independent music scenes in Washington DC and the Pacific Northwest (Washington state) drew inspiration from the Slits. The music was raw and direct (more so, really, than the music of the Slits), and confrontational both in its lyrics and often in their aggressive delivery. But the main difference was in the degree of separatism in the acts that came under the riot grrrl banner: politically, these bands were more developed and more sophisticated in their feminism.

Where the Slits had been part of the British punk wave and indeed inspired by the Sex Pistols (Ari Up's stepfather, in point of fact, was the Pistols' singer, Johnny Rotten), riot grrrl bands such as Bratmobile and Bikini Kill were avowedly independent. They were their own scene; their music and the discourse surrounding it were free from accusations of 'performing masculinity' – none of these singers was trying to be Johnny Rotten or Joey Ramone – but also from traditional conceptions of gender roles and feminine characteristics. (This is in contrast to the intended cover art of Bow Wow Wow's 1981 album, *See Jungle! See Jungle! Go Join Your Gang, Yeah. City All Over! Go Ape Crazy*, which was a photograph of the band posing as the alfresco lunchers in Eduard Manet's painting 'Le déjeuner sur l'herbe', the men fully clothed enjoying a picnic with the naked fifteen-year-old Annabella.)

The riot grrrl bands were fully sexualised – Bikini Kill's 1995 single 'I Like Fucking' is testament to that – but entirely on their own terms. Jack Off Jill, a riot grrrl band from Fort Lauderdale, Florida, released 'Girlscout' (sometimes written as 'Grrl Scout') in 1996, a song that begins rather sweetly, before the chorus turns abruptly into a demanding scream: 'What I want and what I need . . .' It is worth mentioning again that this is not a female performance that draws on stereotypically masculine primitivism, but the creation of an independent feminine primitive in a specific social and musical context.

Punk in any of its forms was unknown in the Soviet Union, and little heard in post-Communist Russia, so the advent in 2011 of Pussy Riot – an all-female band with variable membership – was always likely to attract attention. Inspired by the riot grrrl movement in the United States, and especially by Bikini Kill, the band did not give concerts so much as hit-and-run events, usually lasting just a minute or two. These were filmed, edited, mixed and, in short order, posted on YouTube. You could certainly call the performances primitive – the vocals were seldom in tune and often distorted, the guitars, bass and drums equally basic – but the post-production was slick enough.

More a political movement than a musical one, Pussy Riot's most famous performance was the one that got three of its members gaoled in 2012. Five of these women staged a minute-long performance at the altar of the Russian Orthodox Cathedral of Christ the Saviour in Moscow, which was nearly empty at the time. Beginning rather sweetly (a Pussy Riot trademark) with a chant taken from the 'Ave Maria' in Rakhmaninov's *All Night Vigil*, the resulting video, 'Punk Prayer: Mother of God, Drive Putin Away', continued with an equally typical performance – noisy, messy and full of raw energy – occasionally interrupted by more of the 'Ave Maria'. It was a portmanteau protest against Vladimir Putin (who was up for re-election as president), the patriarchal hierarchy of the Orthodox Church, and the ever-closer ties between Putin and the church.

A few weeks after the performance/protest, Maria Alyokhina, Nadezhda Tolokonnikova and Yekaterina Samutsevich were arrested and eventually tried and sentenced to imprisonment in penal colonies. Putin, meanwhile, introduced new blasphemy laws.

* * *

The use of the singing voice in support of political causes is hardly new; indeed, it is one of the oldest forms of singing. In a way, it is curious that the name Bob Dylan should loom so large in this context, for Dylan was never the political animal he once seemed, and never solely of the left. Dylan was first and last a songwriter, and – inseparable from that fact – the best performer of his own material. Some of his material was political because some of life is political, and also the kinds of singers that the young Dylan admired, such as Woody Guthrie, sang political songs. But Dylan's art was always far broader than the 1960s epithet 'protest singer' would allow.

The other common misunderstanding about Dylan was the widespread belief that he couldn't really sing. In fact, he was an outstanding singer and, for the record, very seldom off-key. Dylan's songwriting was always lyric-driven. He wrote at a typewriter, not at a guitar, and the revelation, in 2014, that there was a sizeable stash of unused song lyrics from Dylan's *Basement Tapes* days in the late 1960s amply demonstrated the point. It also explained why so may of Dylan's early songs were sung to existing tunes, or versions of them: 'Masters of War' used the tune of the traditional English song 'Nottamun Town', 'A Hard Rain's A-Gonna Fall' was modelled on the folk song 'Lord Randall', 'Girl from the North Country' on 'Scarborough Fair'.

For a young songwriter in the throes of prolific creativity, these templates were extremely useful; they also made him part of the tradition that helped form him. But the fact that Dylan was a words-first writer also chimes with his voice. Like those traditional singers before him, like the singers of Africa, Dylan was a storyteller. Vocal beauty had nothing to do with his art; it was above all imperative that the words come across. But when a singer is trying to tell you words, to tell you a story, the music follows, phrasing falls into place, dynamic variety is assured. Particularly when Dylan was singing an angry song, such as 'Masters of War' or 'Maggie's Farm', 'Positively 4th Street' or 'Idiot Wind', he would stress individual words and punch certain syllables in a manner that would shape his whole performance.

Dylan's voice itself went through a number of changes. Early in his career, when he was inventing his persona, he had the wry, gnarly tone of an old farmer (he even looked like one in his overalls); following his motorbike accident in 1966, he came back with a deeper, more conventional voice, quite close to a croon; in the mid-1970s, around the time of *Blood on the Tracks* (1974), the voice became a kind of blend of the first two voices; by the end of the 1980s, when Dylan himself admits (in *Chronicles*) that he was having trouble with his voice, the sound became considerably more nasal; and by the end of the first decade of the twenty-first century, there was really nothing left but a rasp. Throughout, Dylan's approach to singing has been remarkably close to the description of *Sprechstimme* offered by Schoenberg in the preface to the score of *Pierrot lunaire*. Dylan's voice is essentially pitched speech, the notes touched for a moment (and with a strong degree of accuracy), then left for something closer to a spoken tone as the voice moves, sometimes sliding, to the next pitch.

From the 1980s, the sound of speech increasingly came to dominate popular music as rappers put rhythm and rhyme ahead of both singing and melody. But the speaking voice had held a fascination for American composers throughout much of the twentieth century. From Harry Partch to Robert Ashley, Meredith Monk to Laurie Anderson, the music of speech – natural speech, intoned speech, whispering, chanting – was an important inspiration and expressive device. Steve Reich used the speaking voice in a succession of pieces that included *Different Trains* (1988), *City Life* (1995) and *WTC 9/11* (2010), as well as his multimedia works *The Cave* (1990–93) and *Three Tales* (2002). Reich sampled actual speech, analysed it for its melodic content and then selected vocal samples for inclusion in his pieces, the pitches of the voices generating the melodic material of the instruments. In this way, the music of *Different Trains* steps out from the memories of Holocaust survivors, the music of *WTC 9/11* from recordings of air traffic controllers and calls to the New York City Fire Department on 11 September 2001.

The construction of large-scale works from fragments of musical speech can be traced back at least as far as the early sixteenth century when the French composer Clément Janequin composed *Les cris de Paris*, based on the cries of street vendors. Later sets of musical street cries followed in various parts of Europe, but in London around the start of the seventeenth century there was almost a craze for the practice. Some of the strangest and most beguiling examples concoct little scenarios from the assembled cries, placing the voices in counterpoint with a viol consort playing that curiously English piece, the 'In nomine'.

This was a contrapuntal work, almost always for instruments, that had begun with popular transcriptions of the 'in nomine Domini' section from the Benedictus of John Taverner's Mass on the plainsong *Gloria tibi Trinitas* (c. 1530). Throughout the sixteenth century and well into the seventeenth, it was a popular conceit among composers to write new pieces using the same melody, and Orlando Gibbons (1583–1625) was one such. In taking the 'In nomine' as the basis of his two-part composition, *The Cries of London*, he was clearly showing off, but he was also attempting to bring some unity to these disparate cries. Another aspect of this unity was Gibbons's ordering of the calls so as to form an arc stretching from early morning ('God give you good morrow my masters, past three o'clock and a fair morning') to midnight ('Twelve o'clock, look well to your lock, your fire and your light, and so good night'). In between, we encounter the voices of men and women selling everything from 'new lilywhite mussels' and 'oysters, threepence a peck at Bridewell Dock' to 'ripe strawberries' and 'hard onions', along with scurrilous humour about dildos and appeals for 'bread and meat for the poor pris'ners of the Marshalsea, for Christ Jesus' sake'.

We do not really know how these pieces were performed. It seems most likely that they were sung as a domestic entertainment by people who were well acquainted with the calls, just as today we might recognise advertising jingles. However, in modern performances of *The Cries of London* there arises the question of what the singing voices should sound like. These days classical singers, vocal groups and choirs in the United Kingdom sing the English language using 'received pronunciation' (RP) – the standard modern pronunciation of the south-east of England. So do choirs in Australia and New Zealand and, to some degree, in the United States and Canada, though they will pronounce the letter *r* more clearly. But street vendors' cries sung in RP sound absurd.

Some performers, including the Theatre of Voices on their

recording of *The Cries of London*, adopt a speculative semi-rural accent that certainly gives their singing some spirit. But then what about other music of the era? Perhaps the English madrigals of Gibbons, Thomas Morley and Thomas Weelkes were sung in the early-seventeenth-century equivalent of RP. If there ever was such a thing, we don't know how it sounded, though we can be reasonably sure it was not much like modern RP. So should these madrigals also now be sung with a degree of 'ooh arr' in the voice?

This issue became an element in a recent piece by the Australian composer Robert Davidson. Adopting a technique not unlike that used by Reich in *Different Trains*, Davidson had long been interested in taking Australian history, and especially its political history, as a source for his work. To date, he has used speeches by Australian prime ministers from Robert Menzies to Tony Abbott.

A particularly interesting example of this type of work is *Not now, not ever!* (2014), in which a speech delivered in the Australian House of Representatives by the prime minister, Julia Gillard, was turned into a piece for the choir Australian Voices. The speech Davidson chose, from 2012, had received more attention than any other delivered by Gillard, because it was a personal speech that accused the leader of the opposition, Abbott, of sexism and misogyny.

Not now, not ever!, posted on YouTube, received a lot of hits and a lot of media coverage, while the website's comments section predictably unleashed a new wave of sexist and misogynistic remarks. But the internet trolls who attacked the work missed its point (as trolls are wont to do), and so did the right-wing commentators in the press, who seemed incapable of hearing the music.

'The piece,' Davidson explained, 'is primarily a way to paint a portrait, to try and get behind the surface of the words and into the personal emotion conveyed in Gillard's intonation. While I do happen to be very much in agreement with the speech, that would not have to have been the case. This is a storytelling art, not a preaching one.'

Not now, not ever! was unusual among Davidson's political pieces in using a choir, and it presented a particular difficulty. Gillard, as her detractors liked to point out, had a very distinctive voice with a very strong Australian accent. But like most other Australian choirs, Australian Voices typically sings with RP. Davidson decided to turn this to his advantage and indeed make it a feature of the work. At the outset, then, the choir's sound contrasts with Gillard's recorded voice, lending her words a timeless, universal quality. However, towards the end of the four-minute piece, as Gillard suddenly attacks the man opposite her for looking at his watch while she is talking, she speeds up her delivery and shouts. At this moment the women in the choir change their pronunciation to sound like the modern Australians they are, their accents suddenly chiming with Gillard's.

It is the piece's most powerful moment, as it was the most powerful moment of Gillard's speech, and the power comes from the singers' adoption of broad diphthongs and a more nasal tone – the sound not of a modern, Anglophone choir, but of everyday speech and everyday life in Australia.

8

Spiritual Ecstasy and Earthly Desire

An interview with Liza Lim

Liza Lim (born in Perth, Western Australia, in 1966) writes music that is often ritualistic in nature, but always delivers a visceral punch. It is a highly lyrical – indeed ecstatic – music, but unafraid of delving into the darker, uglier side of human nature. Lim has been drawn to many cultures beyond the Western concert hall, including a range of Asian and Aboriginal Australian musical practices. Since 2008, she has been Professor of Composition at the University of Huddersfield, in the United Kingdom. This interview took place in June 2014, between BBC and ABC radio studios in Manchester and Sydney. There was minimal editing.

Andrew Ford: Your piece *The Green Lion Eats the Sun* [2014] is so new that not only have I not heard it, neither have you. But I was interested to read what you wrote about it in a recent blog article, and particularly what you had to say about the conscious and unconscious minds. Is there less will in this piece than in some of your others?

LIZA LIM: That's an interesting question. *The Green Lion Eats the Sun* is a piece for double bell euphonium, a very unusual instrument that Melvyn Poore has developed together with an instrument builder. Basically, there are two bells, so the sound comes out of one bell and then you can switch to the other bell. So it means there is the possibility of having two worlds of colour, really – you can put a mute in one of the bells, you can really divide up the instrument. So it prompted this piece.

I wrote most of it in an airport – a very unpromising location – but it came together in a really unusual and exciting way for me. First, there was the structure of the instrument with these two worlds; then the ideas I wanted to explore, the idea of worlds of consciousness – one side somehow conscious, the other side unconscious, but you could only access one of them at a time through a switch; and then there was my own experience of being in this airport and actually being in a kind of altered state of consciousness, either through boredom or giving in to the situation of a seven-hour delay and deciding to enter into this act of writing of a piece that I'd actually been stuck on. So it was a very unusual moment of breaking through writer's block, the material object of the instrument, certain ideas about the structure of consciousness and then my own state, all coming together in a very particular way.

AF: It sounds to me, because of the nature and location of the process in this case, that there was not much planning in the piece. Does that mean that it's less organised – or less consciously organised – than most of your other pieces?

LL: Well, that's interesting because, as I said, I'd really been stuck on the piece for about two years. I'd been trying to enter into it but just couldn't find any sort of doorway, so it was only on this particular day at Boston Airport that I managed to get into it. So there's an unconscious process, but there was a lot of work at a conscious level before that. Until that day I'd been unable to bring the sides together, this sense of being caught up in the creative flow and more pre-planned, structured ideas. That's the curious thing: you can plan all you like, but you can't necessarily make the creative process flow; it's not there at your bidding all the time.

AF: I get the impression in your music that sound and the quality of sound are paramount. I can't imagine you arranging one of your pieces for other instruments. It seems that every note that you write comes attached to a particular instrument in a particular range, often played by a particular player. Is that your source of inspiration?

LL: Yes. Sonic reality, the fact of vibration in the world, is really important. Imagining the sound in a really concrete way is what actually leads me on, I think, a lot of the time; it's the thread that I follow. There's a sense that the music teaches me ways of listening and thinking as much as my trying to manipulate it.

AF: Let's talk about one of your first pieces – almost a student piece, really – *Garden of Earthly Desire* [1989]. It seems to me that you've been a very consistent composer – this piece already sounds as much like Liza Lim as your more recent pieces – so it makes sense to go back to it. And also it's a good example of the physicality of your music – an early example, but a strong one. Perhaps you could talk about the beginning of that piece: what did you want to usher into being with that oboe?

LL: Oh, gosh. Yes, okay. The beginning of *Garden of Earthly Desire* has this oboe, and again it's like a thread of sound that sets up something for the whole piece. It's the beginning of the journey. It has qualities that recur, I think, in a lot of my music. There's a sense of establishing a point of reference, which is then ornamented and then expands and takes you on a journey. And that's connected to your other question about the quality of sound being important in my music. It's a thing that you hold on to, almost in a physical way. It's something that you travel along. This is one aspect of the embodied and physical quality that I'm looking for in the music that I make – that one can actually be inside it through the qualities of the sound, rather than always having the perspective of being an observer. I want people to have a more immersive relationship to the sound.

AF: And a more visceral response?

LL: Yeah, well . . . It is about physicality, it is about the body. One listens not just with the mind but with the body. The gestural quality of my music invites, perhaps . . . I would like to think . . . sometimes . . . a gesturing within the body as well. It isn't just an intellectual exercise, but is something that can be brought inside the body as a way of listening and understanding and being with the music. And I guess that's a quality that I'm always looking for in any music: you know, this way of being inside the music and living through the music. It's a more interactive experience.

AF: There's also an eroticism to that piece, it seems to me, and quite a lot of your other pieces. I don't know how to explain that, it's just an impression. But is it your impression too?

LL: Um . . . sure! Yes, I mean . . an erotic quality, a visceral quality, a physical sense of entrancement and entrainment . . . It's really a key aspect of what I'm looking for when I'm making music, and also what I'm looking for when I'm listening to other music. The sense of being taken into another state is the erotic as well, this sense of being in the flow, merging with something, being . . . yeah, being in an altered state.

AF: But against that – or maybe it's not against it, maybe it's part of it – there are often quite violent moments, quite violent gestures, quite violent sounds – sounds that come apart, sometimes very beautifully, but sometimes not so beautifully . . .

LL: Yeah . . .

AF: . . . sometimes in a rather worrying way.

LL: Sure.

AF: Is that related to the eroticism, do you think, or is it something different?

LL: Well, I think that element of what you call violence or eroticism, they are connected in that they're about more extreme expressive states. And so, for instance, the quality of distortion that I'm very interested in in music is something that I will connect to heightened emotional states, and that could be in the zone of the erotic or the pleasurable or the joyful, but it could also be in the zone of the painful or the violent or the grieving. I think there is a kind of continuum there. Looking for kinds of expressivity that take you away from the more everyday, medium level of living.

AF: There's also a word that you used when you were talking about *Garden of Earthly Desire*, and that was 'debris'. What did you mean by that? What is musical debris?

LL: [Laughs] I don't remember . . . Yes, debris . . . Well, I had an idea about the structure of *Garden of Earthly Desire*, because, you know, it's quite a long piece. It's half an hour, and it's made up of these multiple sections in which musical materials recur – but they're often fragmented, you only recognise a little bit, because they're broken up and recombined. So the idea of musical debris is perhaps an indicator of the sort of forces that are moving through the music. This is kind of simple, but there is something explosive that results in fragmentation, and there's the attempt to put things back together as well.

AF: Jumping ahead nearly a quarter of a century to *Tongue of the Invisible* [2011], there's an ecstatic quality to that music as well. I know you've described it as a spiritual ecstasy, but do you think it is related to the erotic ecstasy of *Garden of Earthly Desire*?

LL: Sure . . . In *Tongue of the Invisible,* there is the theme of the divine ecstasy: it's based on poems of Hāfez, the great Sufi mystic, and in that Persian Sufi poetic tradition, there's always this really interesting mix between images of earthly eroticism – the lover and the beloved – and at the same time the spiritual. So earthy kinds of metaphors also stand in for spiritual ones; earthly longing is also connected to this longing for the divine. I find that intriguing. I love that kind of fluidity, that ambiguity and shift between different modes – not necessarily staying in one or the other but constantly fluctuating and transforming.

AF: And fluctuating and transforming between the mind and the body in terms of the actual physicality of the music, because often watching your music being performed is quite an important part of the experience. I mean the players: the way they work, the way their bodies are almost choreographed by your music . . .

LL: Well, that is an ideal, that the musicians are so within the experience of playing that there's a merging that goes on there too.

In *Tongue of the Invisible*, I tried to relate some of those Sufi ideas about journeying, wandering, being bewildered, being lost, but also finding something, coming into community, being entranced and finding union as well. I tried to map that to things that the players could also experience, so it wasn't just a description or an illustration of those states, but that they would have experience of wandering and bewilderment and union and community. And I did that by incorporating aspects of relatively open or improvised sections in the work, together with much more structured sections. So there was a real dialogue between composition, offering a way of listening and working with materials, and improvising and elaborating materials for the musicians, and that offering is taken up in various ways. I mean, there's a whole section where the jazz pianist Uri Caine completely improvises but based on a little fragment of a melody. In other parts that melody is something that I've composed out but which is ornamented by other musicians. So there's a sense in which the whole group is this organism, experiencing the music, bringing their own personalities and histories, their own stories to it. And that's part of the piece as well. So that was a really interesting and beautiful project to work on, in the sense of deliberately trying to create this aspect of community.

AF: Do you want the listener to be aware of when the dots stop and the improvising starts, or are you, on the contrary, hoping that the experience of listening to the music will be relatively seamless?

LL: I don't think it matters, really, whether the audience is aware that some things are improvised and others are read from the page. I actually think that everything involves improvisation, even in the most heavily instructed music there's always performer choice, the element of what they bring to it. I don't think you can crush interpretation. But no, I don't think it's necessary for the audience to realise that some sections are improvised and some are scored, but one certainly picks up on different energy levels or different qualities that come with those approaches. And I think that's interesting too. That's part of the texture of the experience.

AF: The musical influences that come from exploring Sufism and Sufi chant, these are things that you've also drawn on, and other vocal techniques from the Middle East – ululation, for instance. What are you hoping to introduce to your music, or perhaps find in your music, by using these techniques, which, after all, come with the resonance of another culture?

LL: In a way, it's not such a deliberate project to create the resonance of Islamic chant in my music. But it totally seeps in, and it's to do with what I've listened to. Different kinds of music – and where I've been when I've listened to it – all come into who I am and then make their way into my music. I think the process is more that there are certain kinds of music that I love, and they ultimately also find their expression in what I'm writing. Certainly in *Tongue of the Invisible* there's this element of a kind of Sufi melisma, a heightened chanting. But it's sung by a

Western-trained opera singer, so it's transformed again – though Omar Ebrahim, the singer, is very aware of those ecstatic vocal traditions and can really get inside that expressive world.

AF: What about your use of Chinese music? Can you describe how that affected your work?

LL: There are lots of different aspects of Chinese culture that I've reflected on in my work: more obvious things like the colourful street operas performed during the Hungry Ghost Festival in Penang, Malaysia, which was the subject of my second opera, *Moon Spirit Feasting* [1997–99], to more hidden aspects of style and gesture that come from the playing tradition of the 'scholar's instrument', the guqin or zither. These interests were kind of reawakened by a recent trip to China. I definitely feel an affinity for both the over-the-top, clashing vibrancy of Chinese performance as well as the more refined, meditative, rather arcane aspects of guqin music.

That was my first trip to mainland China and was so interesting as there's such an obsession with national identity wrapped up in pride for history, with continuity of traditions, desire to assert one's position in the world. My own 'China' is made up of family experiences as part of the migrant diaspora in South-East Asia – that's a rather different place, a hybrid position where identity is made up of perhaps more piecemeal knowledge and things that have travelled and transformed, been forgotten and half-remembered or in some cases, held in quite crystallised ways that belong to a more distant time. But I also get suspicious of this utopian, never-never land of 'tradition'. I get a bit nervous with the rhetoric of 'national identity' as well as 'multiculturalism' that has been such a strong part of the Australian cultural discussion. There's a romanticism there which can all too easily end up in a pretty compromising position with some nasty parts of history – 'tradition' quite often has a past that's in collusion with slavery, genocide, colonialism and so on. The romance of nationalism often denies the ugly parts of history but, more worryingly, turns a blind eye to how that past continues to reach out and affect the present and shape continuing conditions of power. Cultural matters are intimately political!

That, perhaps, explains a bit my attitude to referencing quite diverse cultural materials. Over time, you can see that my work is not just associated with 'Chineseness' or Australian indigenous culture but there's also Sufi mysticism, there are other cultural lineages that I'm drawn to – maybe it gets a bit confusing from a 'branding' point of view . . . There's a certain dynamic of belonging and not-belonging from my own experience that I think I bring to my musical projects. I'm not interested in reproducing tradition but in perhaps showing something of a gap, or where things don't quite add up – it's a modest way of showing that whilst there are analogies and linkages between many things, there's no totalising essence. I'm going for relationship and conversation with everything – or another way to put it is to say that 'otherness' and 'sameness' are constantly transforming in their meanings and qualities.

AF: It occurs to me that perhaps you don't agree with my earlier assertion that your music is very consistent. Maybe you think of each of your works as a new beginning. Is that true, or do you see a thread that runs through everything?

LL: I do see a thread. And when I look at what appear to be a great diversity of interests and projects – whether it's aspects of Chinese music, and particularly ritual music, my interest in Aboriginal culture, and very recently writing a piece for the Norwegian Hardanger fiddle and being interested in Nordic stories – what brings them together is the broader theme of ways of looking at the world which are non-mechanistic, a body-knowledge that can only be passed down through experience and an oral tradition.

AF: The other piece I particularly want to ask you about, because I suspect it's a really important one for you, is *Songs Found in Dream* [2005]. It seems to me to be a summing up, for the time being at least, of your experience of Aboriginal culture – which is reasonably extensive, isn't it?

LL: Well, *Songs Found in Dream* was a work written about ten years ago, and it was connected to some quite intense explorations and journeyings to meet artists in Aboriginal communities, and just learning a little bit more about the culture and philosophy and aesthetics, and being totally blown away by the richness and extraordinariness, particularly of Yolngu culture in the north-east part of Arnhem Land. *Songs Found in Dream* was one piece in which I tried to touch aspects of that experience, not through any direct quotations – there's no element of Aboriginal songs in it, or even rhythms – but there's a certain quality of vibrancy I was looking for. And a quality of layers, in which many layers veil other layers and then come apart and show something else, this element of veiling and revelation which is such an extraordinary and fascinating part of that culture up north. So it was a way of processing and also wanting to bring that into myself and into my creative process.

AF: The title alone seems to describe a part of that process, but it also brings us back to *The Green Lion Eats the Sun* – those two sides, the conscious and unconscious sides of creativity.

LL: Yes, I adore that Aboriginal concept of songs found in dream. There are actually various words – in fact, a whole vocabulary – to describe something which is found in dream or, let's say, in non-ordinary reality, altered states of consciousness. I love the idea that one would find valuable knowledge or creative power in those states. In Western culture we substitute the word 'dreamtime' to talk about this creative presence in Aboriginal thinking. It's this idea that you don't construct something, but that you stalk it, you hunt it, you hunt creative knowledge in those states. I think that's found in quite a few indigenous cultures. That's where music comes from, that's where art comes from. It's not something one can make in a purely intellectual way; it relies on another state of consciousness.

9

Droning On

Walk so silently that the bottoms of your feet become ears.

Pauline Oliveros

Drones have got themselves a bad name. The musical term presumably derives from the unwavering buzz of the bee, specifically
the male honey bee or drone (from the Anglo-Saxon *drǽn*), which
is distinguished from other bees by its essential uselessness: beyond
being on call to fertilise a receptive queen, drones do no work and
make no honey; they just hang around in groups, permanently
out to stud. Perhaps this is why P.G. Wodehouse invented the
Drones Club for Bertie Wooster and his friends, none of whom
has a real job; or perhaps he was thinking of another meaning of
the word: a bore, who talks on endlessly like a musical drone.
Boredom is probably the most common negative association of
the word, but if you add to the list of usages those from modern
warfare – remotely piloted aircraft dropping bombs on military
targets and unarmed civilians alike – you end up with a thoroughly
unattractive concept. Yet drones or *bourdons* (the French word is
also bee-related) underpin much of the world's music, sounding
on and on while other things happen above and around them.

* * *

The opening bars of Gustav Mahler's Symphony No 1 never fail to radiate a glacial balm. At the threshold of audibility, the double basses, divided in three, sound their low A, the A above it, and the A above that. The upper As are both harmonics. Divided cellos play the next three As, also as harmonics, their top note reinforced by the violas in unison, while all the violins play the A harmonic above that – the one at the top of the piano keyboard. That's seven octaves of As, shimmering gently, but it is the lowest note that is significant. Mahler, in an instruction to the conductor, insists that, though played softly, this bottom A must be *sehr deutlich* – 'very clear'.

Just as the first symphony of Brahms owed a debt to Beethoven's ninth, so does the opening of Mahler's first. At the start of Beethoven's symphony, the sustained A is less radiant and more of a dark rumble. It is also heard with its dominant E. On top of this, the violins play a succession of falling perfect fifths (E to A) and fourths (A to E). Beethoven's symphony is in D minor, so this introductory passage is in the dominant A major/minor. It lasts approximately thirty seconds, all the time swelling in volume and busyness, and is really a big upbeat to the main action.

Mahler's symphony is in D major, so from a harmonic point of view the same upbeat analogy applies, but in this introduction the double basses' low A will sound – with and without the upper harmonics – for a little over four minutes, heavy with atmosphere, pregnant with intent. The only precedent for this was Wagner's sustained E flat at the outset of *Das Rheingold*, which is also the outset of *Der Ring des Nibelungen*. There is something about beginning a piece with so much harmonic stasis that lets us know in advance that we are in for a long journey – in Wagner's case, approximately sixteen hours over four nights. Mahler's symphony only lasts about fifty minutes, which by 1888 was no longer an extreme duration for a symphony, and what is notable is the fact that the sustained A occupies a full quarter of that first movement, and indeed about eight per cent of the entire work. This was certainly something more than the traditional slow introduction that had begun symphonies since Haydn's day.

Above the A, Mahler gives us falling perfects fourths, as in the Beethoven, but where in Beethoven's ninth they were agitated, here they are slowly and gently played by a woodwind chorale, and they are extended melodically. Next, a pair of clarinets plays distant horn calls. Are these echoes of hunting horns? Tennyson's 'horns of Elfland faintly blowing'? Then – literally in the distance – trumpet fanfares reach us from way off-stage. They seem vaguely regal in character, or possibly military. Then, suddenly, spotlit, there's a cuckoo – Mahler actually names the bird in the score – a solo clarinet with that same falling fourth, but faster and spikier.

In an early program note, cajoled from its composer by his publisher, Mahler spoke of this introduction in terms of the 'awakening of nature', but his audiences hardly needed this pointed out to them. It is apparent from the start that we are in the natural world, probably in one of those magical Germanic forests so beloved of the Romantic artist. A cuckoo, hunters or elves, the palace – or an army – in the extreme distance: it is scene-setting on a grand scale, a painted backdrop, dramatically lit. And supporting it all, there's that drone.

Scotland's Great Highland bagpipe is the world's most familiar drone instrument, found nearly everywhere. It has a bag with a blow pipe to inflate it, a chanter (which is to say a pipe with finger holes for playing melodic lines – a bit like a recorder), and three more pipes that produce only drones – two tenor drones and one bass. Military pipe bands were ubiquitous during the heyday of the British Empire, and they have remained unaccountably popular since. You can find pipe bands in parts of the Middle East and in Thailand. But the instrument that gave the world 'Bonnie Dundee' and 'Scotland the Brave' is only one example of an extended family that stretches across Europe and beyond. There are fifteen or sixteen types of bagpipe in the British Isles alone, and still more in France; bagpipes are found in Scandinavia, all around the Mediterranean and the Balkans, and can be heard in parts of Saharan Africa and the south of India. All these instruments have drones and, in some cases, little more. For example, the śruti-upanga, found in Tamil Nadu, is used exclusively to provide a drone to accompany the mukha-vina, a double-reed melody instrument that is a bit like an oboe.

We may speculate about the origin of the drone. For instance, it is tempting to say something about those flat, unchanging pitches representing the earth, from which melody emerges to fly free. It is a perfectly serviceable analogy, though whether our ancestors thought in those terms is anyone's guess. What is beyond doubt is that composers who have drawn on folk music have often romanticised it in this way. They bring a drone into their work so as to add a touch of rusticity. Certainly, the audience that first heard Beethoven's *Pastoral* symphony would not have missed the reference. The low strings' sustained F and C may be short-lived, but it is the first thing we hear in the piece, and its symbolism would have been lost on no one.

Similarly, listeners to Corelli's Concerto grosso in G minor, Op 6, No 8 (1690), commonly known as the 'Christmas' concerto, would have needed no telling that the final movement was about shepherds, and the Dublin audience that attended the first performance of Handel's *Messiah* (1742) would have spotted the same shepherds the moment the drone started up at the beginning of the minute-long 'Pastoral Symphony' that ushers in the Christmas music. It is exactly the same in Mahler's first symphony, where we do not have to wait for the hunting horns or the cuckoo in order to know we are in the country: that long-held A tells us instantly that this is a pastoral moment.

In fact, in Mahler, the moment is more than simply pastoral. The 'awakening of nature' of which Mahler spoke was not a dawn chorus or even the coming of spring – it was the very first 'awakening of nature' at the dawn of time. The drone mirrors this. It is Ur-music: not only is nature being born, but so is melody, so is harmony. And when Mahler's four minutes of A are over and the orchestra launches into its big first-subject theme in the tonic D major, we feel a release of tension brought on by a four-minute upbeat. The tune we hear is a wordless version of the second song from Mahler's cycle *Lieder eines fahrenden Gesellen* ('Songs of a

Wayfarer'), in which that Romantic archetype, the wanderer, strides out one morning to bask in nature, as a cheery finch and a bluebell call out to him, 'Isn't it a wonderful world!' (Even a German Romantic must be wary of talking birds and flowers.)

In the final number of *Winterreise* (1828), Schubert's great song cycle turned mad scene, another wanderer meets an old hurdy-gurdy player. Wilhelm Müller's poem 'Der Leiermann' ('The Hurdy-Gurdy Man' or 'The Organ-grinder') has a sluggish feel to it. The diction is *staccato*, made up of short words of one or two syllables, and each couplet is a weary trudge to a standstill.

> Barfuß auf dem Eise
> Schwankt er hin und her;
> Und sein kleiner Teller
> Bleibt ihm immer leer.
>
> Keiner mag ihn hören,
> Keiner sieht ihn an;
> Und die Hunde brummen
> Um den alten Mann.

The old man stands barefoot in the snow. No one is listening to his hurdy-gurdy, no one speaks to him, there are no coins on his plate, and dogs growl at his feet. The wanderer – a jilted lover, no longer in his right mind – stares blankly at the hurdy-gurdy man. Perhaps he should follow him; maybe he will play the wanderer's songs too. To these images of utter desolation Schubert adds the drone of the hurdy-gurdy – throughout the song, the pianist's left hand sticks to its open fifth of B and F sharp – supplying a simple tune for the singer to match the dull tread of Müller's words. Only the right hand of the piano accompaniment attempts something more, with simple melodic arabesques that seem to want to break free of the drone, but must always return to the tonic B. The song is poignant and very beautiful, but we feel trapped by the music and helpless.

* * *

In popular music, the drone plays many of the same roles as in classical music. It might not be intended to transport us to a pastoral idyll, but it often takes us to a place where the musician and listener may feel there is something authentic occurring. This is because many blues songs either employ a single chord or can be sung above an unchanging bass note. To take an example that has already been mentioned, Muddy Waters's 'Mannish Boy' bolsters the blunt insistence of its lyric by an unwavering bass riff that rises a minor third then falls stepwise back to the tonic A. In fact, you could sound the tonic from the start of the song to the end.

Muddy Waters co-composed 'Mannish Boy' with Bo Diddley, and he was another performer with little need of modulation. Just as Bo Diddley's syncopated beat runs unswervingly through his songs, so the harmonic template is generally limited to a drone. 'Hey, Bo Diddley', 'Pretty Thing', 'Who Do You Love?': they all adhered to the pattern, and the drone formed part of an act that emphasised the Southern, if not African, roots of this music and its raw authenticity. At first glance, his oblong-shaped guitar might have been one he had knocked together himself from an old box; in some accounts, even his name was a reference to the 'diddley bow', a primitive, homemade slide guitar with just a single string that was often the blues musician's first childhood instrument.

In contrast to the diddley bow, the Indian sarangi has thirty-eight or forty strings, but only three that are actually bowed. The others are known as sympathetic strings, tuned so as to ring out (in sympathy) when their pitch is sounded on a bowed string. Among the world's folk instruments, drones are often generated or embellished by the resonance from such strings, the effect that of a subtly fluctuating halo of sound. There are sympathetic strings on the Swedish nyckelharpa and the Norwegian Hardanger fiddle, and on the hurdy-gurdy. The zither (of which the world has hundreds of sorts) works similarly, because any strings that are not being plucked or struck become, by default, sympathetic. Practically all Indian stringed instruments – the sitar and surbahar, the sarod, the esraj and dildruba – have this extra resonance from sympathetic strings. Even the harmonium, a somewhat controversial instrument in Indian music because of its inability to bend pitch, provides evidence that if an instrument remains in India long enough, someone will add sympathetic strings to it: the samvadini is a harmonium with a box of strings.

The classical music of India is entirely drone-based, the constant pitch generally produced by the open strings of a tanpura (or tambura), a long-necked instrument tuned to the tonic in various octaves with an added fifth or sometimes fourth, though these days it is also relatively common to see a smartphone app in use. Because of its ever-present drone, some would argue the music is, by definition, non-harmonic, but this is not strictly accurate. It is true that there are no chord changes in Indian music, no modulation and no harmonic development, but that is not to say there is an absence of harmonic tension. On the contrary, in Indian music – as in many other drone-based forms of music – the tension is generated by the relationship of the melodic line to the constant drone. Some of the notes in the raga will be more dissonant than others, pulling against the 'tonic' of the bass, while the expressive use of bent quarter-tones, typical of Indian music (whether sung, blown or plucked), heightens the tension in a way that can really only be heard harmonically. The presence of sympathetic strings enhances the quasi-harmonic feel of the music, in that they will cause other notes of the raga to hang in the air.

The system of ragas in Hindustani and Carnatic music is ancient, complex and immensely rich. At one level, a raga is merely a scale or mode, but it is also much more than that. For one thing, some ragas contain the same notes as each other. It is to do with mood as much as anything else; in the northern Hindustani tradition, individual ragas are associated with different seasons or times of day. Playing an evening raga in the middle of the morning would be unthinkable. The drone in Indian classical music serves to ground the raga. It is a support, a reference point from which all else proceeds, the foundation for a musical exploration that may last more than an hour and be extremely complex. And yet in Western classical music, with its preference for harmonic development, the drone always seems to represent something basic and primitive, or at least rustic.

* * *

The idea of music consisting of little more than drones caught on in the early 1960s in San Francisco, when composers including La Monte Young and Pauline Oliveros – minimalists *avant la lettre* – began listening to sustained tones, the musical interest coming from subtle changes of pitch or timbre, the way in which notes decayed and were renewed. It is no coincidence that Stockhausen composed *Stimmung* (1968) following a sojourn in the Bay Area – and during the 'summer of love', what is more. From a harmonic point of view, *Stimmung* is static. For anywhere between an hour and ninety minutes, six closely miked singers vocalise very quietly on a single chord based on the overtones of a low B flat, these notes in turn forming the fundamentals for harmonic singing. The B flat drone, then, is the source of every pitch in the piece; even when not being sung by the bass voice, it stays in the memory of the listener.

Many of the early pieces by Terry Riley, Steve Reich and Philip Glass also had their origins in this sort of thinking. Glass's *Music with Changing Parts* (1970) is constructed around long-sustained drones from wind instruments and voices; Reich's pioneering tape-loop pieces *It's Gonna Rain* (1965) and *Come Out* (1966) both end up as drones. Each of Reich's phrases commences from fragments of recorded speech – in both cases it's a rather emotional speaker –

before the looped voice, running on two tape machines, begins slowly to get out of phase with itself. As this happens, the clarity of the voice is slowly lost. In *Come Out*, the phasing effect is doubled, then redoubled, the final result a buzzing continuum of tone.

Drone music became (somewhat) more commercial with Brian Eno. Long interested in a range of music beyond his work with Roxy Music, Eno was one of the first composers to experiment seriously with music as ambience. It is very easy to dismiss this music as 'classical muzak', because in a way that's what it is. Eno's ambient pieces, like Erik Satie's 'Furniture Music', succeed only if one is able to ignore them. But unlike Satie, Eno was also keen that people should be able to listen as and when they wanted. Eno's ideal was music that would run on, allowing people to tune in and out at will. The drone, then, was a good starting point, and in pieces such as 'The Heavenly Music Corporation' from *No Pussy-footing*, Eno's 1973 album with Robert Fripp, the drone, with attendant overtones, is all.

More recent manifestations of drone music have been considerably less ambient. 'Drone metal' – sometimes called 'drone doom' – really began at the start of the 1990s in Seattle, when guitarist Dylan Carlson formed his band, Earth, purveyors, at least initially, of loud, slow, repetitive grungy distortion, based on a single continuous and very low pitch. Their first (live) album, *Extra-Capsular Extraction* (1991), featured the voice of Kurt Cobain on one track, but the basic Earth sound was instrumental, consisting of guitar, bass and drums. The tracks were long – the first studio album, *Earth 2*, runs for seventy-five minutes and contains just three tracks – and the mood dark. Later albums included *Phase 3: Thrones and Dominions* (1995) and *Pentastar: In the Style of Demons* (1996), titles suggesting that it was the witches-and-wizards end of metal from which this music had emerged, and the Dungeons and Dragons end of the market at which it was aimed.

Other Seattle drone doom bands included Goatsnake and Burning Witch, one member from each forming the highly influential duo Sunn O))), who always performed dressed in black monks' robes. To be a fan of drone doom, then, you had to buy into the mythology to some extent (of course that's also true of Wagner), but there was important work going on here, across a range of musical genres. Earth's later albums increasingly took them down some unexpected paths into country music and English folk song; in 2014, Sunn O))) made a studio album, *Soused*, with Scott Walker; other favoured collaborators were the Japanese noise artist Merzbow and the Australian Oren Ambarchi.

One concert-hall composer who used drones throughout his career was the Australian Peter Sculthorpe (1929–2014), and the end result of this in his work was particularly interesting. Strictly speaking, Sculthorpe's drones were pedal points, the main difference between the two being their length. In harmonic music, a pedal point is a bass note that continues to sound even as the harmony above it shifts. The result is generally a dissonance – the old bass against the new harmony – which is then resolved. It is a bit like a suspension, except that with a suspension the sustained tone is usually higher than the moving harmony, and the note that hangs over resolves to the new chord. In contrast, pedal points hold their own, pulling the dissonant harmony back to them, which is why they more closely resemble drones. In Sculthorpe's music, the pedals and the harmonic tension can carry over sometimes for minutes on end.

There is nothing especially noteworthy about pedal points: they are everywhere in music. Mahler used them, Sibelius made extensive use of them, and, as already observed, they are beloved by heavy metal bands. But the interesting thing about Sculthorpe's pedals is what they later made possible. Sculthorpe's orchestral pieces *Mangrove* (1979), *Earth Cry* (1986) and *Kakadu* (1988) were already among his best-known works when, at the end of the twentieth century, he began to reconsider the scores, in each case adding a didgeridoo to the instrumentation.

The Aboriginal didgeridoo is a drone instrument that builds its music from rhythm and from the often virtuosic use of overtones. Sculthorpe's didgeridoo player of choice was William Barton, an indigenous man from Mount Isa, in Queensland. But the composer didn't write parts for Barton; he simply allowed him to play along with the pieces. The extraordinary thing about the collaboration was not just that Barton seemed instinctively to know what was needed, but also that these works accepted his contributions so readily. The long pedal points in the scores accommodated Barton and his didgeridoo almost as though the works had, hitherto, been incomplete and were only now properly finished.

Sculthorpe's music has frequently been spoken of in terms of landscape, and in discussing his work in later years, Sculthorpe himself came to adopt the imagery of the wide, flat outback reflected in the often slow pace of his music, the narrow range of his melodic lines and, above all, the slow rate of harmonic change associated with these pedal points. The Western Australian composer Alan Lamb went a stage further, stepping into the outback itself and even allowing it to make its own music. Lamb takes recording equipment on his trips in order to capture the music of the wind in telegraph wires. In 2000 he described the experience of making these recordings:

'The landscape that I think of is where I did most of my early music, down at the Great Southern region of Western Australia, bordering on the outback. It's quite high and flat, the sort of place where you can see weather coming twenty-four hours in advance, and see it disappearing over the other horizon twenty-four hours later . . . It undulates, it reminds me of the ocean . . . It's very wild, remote and huge, and you can *feel* it. It's much more than what goes through your eyes and ears. I find it very mystical, in a way.'

The music of the wires – Lamb calls it 'singing' – consists, usually, of a constant drone above and around which long, slow changes of overtones build and dissipate. But there are also sudden noises that sound like cymbal crashes. Lamb has a day job as a general practitioner in Perth; he is a man of science, but the sound of the wires would be enough to make anyone feel mystical.

'There's no doubt at all that the telegraph wires and the music I've recorded from them are responding in some way to the elements of the landscape,' Lamb explained. 'There are two levels of looking at this. One is that the shape of the landscape itself, the directions of the winds, the climate have an obvious physical effect on the winds that create the music in the wires. But there is something else, too, about the importance of landscape, and I think it comes back to this mysterious extra quality. I've been trying for years to work this one out. It's almost as if the wires have become imbued by the spirit of the place. There are times when I've heard the wires singing and there's really been no reason for it – no *obvious* reason. You can feel that the atmosphere is vibrating, and yet there may be no wind at all. I've heard the most extraordinary sound under these conditions, so there is some kind of peculiar interaction going on at a level that I've never truly worked out.'

Drones in the music of Sculthorpe and Lamb have come to represent the large expanses of the Australian outback as surely as they stood for nature in the music of European Romantics, shepherds – especially shepherds at the Nativity – for baroque composers, and the crack of doom for drone metal bands. In each case, it is something primitive, something fundamental that we feel through our feet – a continuum capable of giving rise to elaborate melodic lines and of supporting them, but also capable of just being still and drawing us in.

10

Deep Listening

AN INTERVIEW WITH PAULINE OLIVEROS

Pauline Oliveros (born in Houston, Texas, in 1932) is a composer, improviser and accordionist. She is a vital figure in experimental music, especially as a collaborator with other instrumentalists and artists. She was also a pioneer in the area of electronic music while at the San Francisco Tape Music Center in the early 1960s. Most of her music since those days has been based on drones, and is not notated in any conventional manner. She makes much use of the acoustics in which she performs, favouring resonant spaces in which the listener will feel immersed in the sound of her accordion. The interview was conducted over Skype in July 2014.

ANDREW FORD: When did you first hold an accordion?

PAULINE OLIVEROS: When I was nine years old. My mother brought home an accordion, and she wanted to learn so she could increase her income. She was a pianist, and the accordion was very popular at that time, so she brought one home and I got fascinated with it.

AF: How long was it before you began to play the way you do now?

PO: The teacher I had introduced me to Bach organ works and I was playing whatever kind of literature could be transcribed. But I found it a fascinating instrument. It had a keyboard, which was somewhat familiar because of my piano-playing mother and grand-mother. But I think I just liked the sound of it.

AF: I think you also played the tuba and the French horn?

PO: Yes, but this was later, when I entered middle-level school – junior high school. The accordion wasn't something that could be played in the band, and so I was given a tuba and a book and sent off into a room by myself to learn it.

AF: Perhaps this is just rationalising, but it seems to make sense that these are all instruments you breathe through . . .

PO: Wind instruments, right . . .

AF: Even the accordion has wind going through it . . .

PO: Right.

AF: And there's a fit there with your music today. It continues right through to your collaboration with Stuart Dempster . . .

PO: Of course, yes. But when I started composing, I was composing at the piano and I was writing pieces for piano and other instruments – piano and violin, and I remember doing a wind quintet, and a piece for horn and harp – these were very early pieces. So I wasn't writing for the accordion in the beginning.

AF: So when did the accordion become an extension of your musical personality?

PO: Well, when I was working with the San Francisco Tape Music Center, working with tape music and then electronic music; we were also doing improvisation. The first improvisation we did, I used the horn, I wasn't using my accordion, but then later on – probably around 1960 – I began to do improvisation with the accordion.

AF: What did the people at the San Francisco Tape Music Center have in common – Morton Subotnick, Ramon Sender, Terry Riley, yourself?

PO: It was a community of artists that kept expanding. What we had in common was our interest in tape and electronic music – and new music in general, because all of us were composing for instruments as well as making tape and electronic music. Each person was quite individual and different, but the common interest was in that edge of making music that wasn't fitting in to the universities at the time, or necessarily into establishment concerts, so we made our own.

AF: So it was political as well?

PO: Oh, it's always political [laughs].

AF: Can we talk about drones? Because this is where that interest began for you, I think, with some of your early tape pieces.

PO: Well, the first drone piece that I did was called *Light Piece for David Tudor* [1965], and I made a piece that consisted of a number of tape loops of the tone D flat – I mean D flat on the middle line of the bass clef – and we had a series of Ampex PR-10 tape machines, so I could set up a number of loops and have them run simultaneously. My *intention* was to have those loops run simultaneously and to create standing waves, but that was something that I found out wasn't feasible because they didn't all run at the same speed. So that was a different kind of drone than I had expected. And David was also playing D flat – his only instruction was to play D flat, and he played it every which way, which was wonderful – so the piece worked, even though the intention or the conception didn't work just because of the mechanics of the machines.

AF: Did you feel at the time that this was a good thing or a bad thing?

PO: It was just how it was.

AF: What is it about drones that appeals to you? Are you able to put it into words?

PO: Well, I was interested in the sound of a single tone . . . which was not single. It was always interesting to listen to because there was so *much* to listen to. People were so fixed on melody and harmony and rhythm – they were forgetting to listen to the quality of the sound. And that's what I was interested in. And that's what you get when you are dealing with drones. You get quality, and you begin to understand it in a more vertical way than the horizontal movement of, say, melody – although you begin to hear that, as well. So there's a lot to listen to.

AF: The figure of John Cage of course looms when you speak like that. His very inclusive way of being has been yours as well. Did you find you had a lot in common with Cage?

PO: Well, in some respects, not all. I met David Tudor in 1963, and David was more influential, as far as I'm concerned. We curated a festival in 1964, with the music of Cage and Toshi Ichiyanagi, Alvin Lucier and myself. Cage happened to come through San Francisco and came to the festival, which was really wonderful. That's when I first met him, when he attended the festival. And it was also kind of healing for Cage, because he had just had his piece *Atlas Eclipticalis* [1961–62] sabotaged by the New York

Philharmonic and their really juvenile behaviour. And we played it – we played *Atlas Eclipticalis* at the festival under the tutelage of David Tudor, and it was really quite a beautiful performance – and so he got to hear it how it was supposed to be!

AF: Perhaps we can come to the concept of 'deep listening'. The business of listening is something that Cage always stressed, and what you're talking about is similar, in a way, in that it involves listening to everything.

PO: Yes, of course, inclusive listening – but it also involves exclusive listening and the balancing of the two forms. What happens when we are born into this world is that we've already been listening from the womb and listening to quite a lot of sounds, but we're also hearing speech, and when we do come into the world we are ready to listen to speech – we're optimised for speech. Eventually, instead of having trillions of neurons, they get sloughed off because we're not using them any more, so our listening becomes more exclusively for communication. Meanwhile, there's all of these other things going on. The life of the environment. In my case, it was incredibly rich in terms of all kinds of sounds from the sentient world – I mean insects, birds, animals and whatever – and I liked to listen to that. And I also liked to listen to the sounds of motors in cars, which were very different in the 1930s than they are now. I was always fascinated with whatever I could hear.

And so I listened inclusively as well as exclusively. I learnt how to talk and express myself and communicate, but I never lost interest in the environment, in the sounds around me. So you're asking me about deep listening: this is my practice of listening and also of imparting my practice to others. But when you ask me what *is* listening, what I'm saying these days is, 'I don't know.' I don't think that we know what listening is any more than we know what consciousness is. When you hear someone say, 'Listen!', they're really calling your attention to exclusive listening; they're not calling your attention to inclusive listening. My interest is in getting auditory neuroscientists really invested in examining what is listening. What *is* it? I'm sure I don't know. [Laughs]

AF: When I listen to your music, the word 'deep' seems to have more than one meaning in the context of 'deep listening'. There is always something very rich and sonorous about the combination of accordion and trombone, say. It seems to be deep in that sense, and it's almost as though the music is drawing you into its depths.

PO: Well, why not? Certainly, when we made the recording in the cistern in 1988 – which is where the words 'deep listening' come from . . . It was partly a pun, because we were fourteen feet underground. So when we said 'deep listening', we were laughing. Are you familiar with the recording, *Deep Listening* [1989]?

AF: Yes, that's what I was thinking of.

PO: We had to listen to ourselves, we had to listen to each other and we also had to listen to the cistern and its myriad reflections of sound that were coming back to us with a forty-five-second reverberation time – which was very unusual, to say the least!

AF: That gave it even more depth!

PO: Definitely, yes, of course it did!

AF: Can we go back to your piece *Sound Patterns* [1961]? It was a groundbreaking work in many ways, one of which was that a piece for chorus didn't use text but phonetic sounds. Texts were replaced by timbre, really.

PO: Yes.

AF: Was this piece at a crossroads for you? Because although it was a strictly notated piece, the sound of it seems to point towards everything that followed.

PO: Yes, I think that's true. This piece won the Gaudeamus Prize in 1962, and the judge was György Ligeti. He told me that it was a very original piece, and it was after this that he wrote *Aventures* [1963]. So it was recognised at that time.

AF: A lot of composers having had a success like that would have stuck with it, but *Sound Patterns* was one of your last notated pieces.

PO: There was also *Outline* for flute, percussion and string bass [1963], Trio for Flute, Piano and Page Turner [1961], Variations for Sextet [1960], so I had a good amount of notated pieces, but I was on my way to dispensing with conventional notation, for sure.

AF: Did you feel that it was a matter of freeing yourself from notation, or was it a way of becoming more expressive?

PO: Well, both. The fact is that the notation system that we have is mostly centred on pitch and rhythm. There's dynamic and articulation, but there's really no way of notating timbral considerations in that system, or only a very limited way. And also I was moving into working with electronics and tape music – tape music first, then electronic music – where I didn't need to notate, so I was freed from the notational system simply by working with tape, though there were other limitations that I had to work with and overcome. So it's just been a continual evolution of learning how to make the music that I want to make.

AF: I've been listening again recently to *Crone Music* and *The Roots of the Moment*, both of which are associated with that Mabou Mines production of *King Lear* [actually called simply *Mabou Mines Lear*]. When someone asks you to be part of a project like that – and there's more to the job than simply listening to the music in your head, there's a whole other text – does that change the way you work?

PO: Well, the first track on *Deep Listening* is called 'Lear', and New Albion released that CD in 1989. *Mabou Mines Lear* wasn't until 1991, I think [1990, in fact.]. So I don't know how that happened.

AF: Perhaps it was the *Deep Listening* track that commended you to Mabou Mines for that project.

PO: No, I'd known Lee Breuer since 1960, and it was clear he wanted to work with me. I liked the project because the gender roles were reversed, which was very interesting to have Lear played by a woman instead of a man, for example – but all of the roles were reversed, which gave it a very different slant.

AF: Did you take the text into account?

PO: I was listening to the sound of the text and picking up the emotional underpinnings of what was being said. Lee wanted to have music all the way through, which was also very unusual, because usually music is like a sideline . . . it doesn't have a through line, but in this case it did. So it made for a very rich production, because the music was always there. And I had already done that music. I had made the recordings of *The Roots of the Moment* and also the recording of 'Lear', and so it was a matter of placing that music with the production, and also some sounds that were wanted. One of my great regrets is that there is not any real recording of the whole thing. I wish there were.

AF: The words that keep coming up in reading and thinking about you and your music are 'composition', 'improvisation', 'meditation' and 'ritual'. Are they in some senses interchangeable?

PO: No, I don't think so.

AF: So then how do they relate? Because they're all aspects of what you do, aren't they?

PO: Possibly, yes. But the concerts I play these days are all improvised. There's nothing written. Deep listening is a form of meditation, and that is my practice, so I'm always involved with that practice. So if I'm going to perform, that's what I'm doing: I'm practising deep listening, and the improvisation comes from that. So it's not necessarily interchangeable, but it is symbiotic, I would say.

AF: You can do deep listening without improvising, but you can't improvise without deep listening.

PO: Well . . . Maybe that's right.

AF: And what about the fourth word, 'ritual': what does that mean to you?

PO: That's harder to explain, I think, because it's a word that's been put on what I'm doing. But for any concert performance there's a concert ritual: how the stage is set; how the performers are arranged; if there's a conductor, how the conductor comes on and takes position and works with the players. Those are all forms of ritual, things that are repeated in a concert. My ritual might be that I come on stage, acknowledge the audience, sit down, pick up my accordion, and then I usually blow air through the instrument. So I think of ritual as some form of action that is repeated.

AF: What would you say music is for?

PO: Well . . . I don't know [laughs]. I don't know what it's for. It's like I don't know what listening is. Why does it have to be for something? It just is. We don't know where it came from, it just happened. It is part of our lives. It is an amazing gift, to have music and to be able to take part in it. Why or how that is, or what it is for . . . It's for expanding one's mind.

11

Child's Play

. . . sullen peoples
Half-devil and half-child.

'The White Man's Burden', Rudyard Kipling

One Sunday teatime in December 1957, CBS television transmitted live from one of its studios in New York City an hour-long program, *The Sound of Jazz*. For all sorts of reasons, the film remains uniquely important. For a start, there's Count Basie's benign swagger as he steers his band through 'Open All Night'; there's Coleman Hawkins, a tenor skylark issuing a stream of melodic invention; there's Gerry Mulligan, all college-boy looks and chequered coat, like a copywriter from *Mad Men*; and, so memorably, so touchingly, there's the final performance together by Billie Holiday and Lester Young (it was actually the last time they would even see each other). There are also some nice moments of unintentional humour, mostly attending the cool-cat earnestness of the critic John Crosby, who presents the hour. But among all these riches, it's Thelonious Monk's performance that still pulls you up short.

From his first notes, we find ourselves in another world – a world in which chains of major and minor thirds replace the swinging, blues-rooted music of the previous numbers. In actual fact, the structure of 'Blue Monk' is that of a twelve-bar blues, but you could be forgiven for missing this as those ubiquitous rising thirds sharpen the harmony, continually lining up to deliver major chords where, in classic blues, one would expect minor chords. The typically flattened thirds, fifths and sevenths of the standard blues are all raised in 'Blue Monk'. But that's not the shock; that's a breath of fresh air.

The shock is delivered by Monk's piano playing. After Hawkins, Mulligan, Ben Webster and Red Allen have made light of their techniques, delivering evident virtuosity with nonchalant ease, Monk's flat-fingered stabbing seems oafish, his awkwardness mirroring John Crosby's struggle in his introduction to pronounce the name of the Monk trio's bassist, Ahmed Abdul-Malik.

Of course, this is about appearance as much as anything. The first chorus of 'Blue Monk' – the head – is played simply enough, but then, as the camera moves in close on the keyboard, Monk's approach changes. Perhaps he is aware that now we can see his fingers; perhaps he is exaggerating for the benefit of those early-evening viewers. In any case, suddenly we are hearing jerky, dislocated rhythm, heavy stresses falling on unexpected parts of the melody, dissonances so seemingly random that they sound like wrong notes. We are seeing Monk's straight, stiff fingers striking the keys like a two-finger typist, the same finger stabbing consecutive notes of a melody.

The thing to say straight away about Monk is that he was fully in command of his technique. There can be no doubt that he knew what he was doing: it might look unschooled, but he was perfectly aware, for example, that the use of single stiff fingers (which in any case was only one part of his technical armoury) would force him to articulate a melodic line with not a hint of *legato*, and this, much of the time, was his aim. It was the same when he divided a melodic line between two hands – a way of ensuring disjuncture.

The poet and jazz critic Philip Larkin was not a fan of Monk. More generally, he was not a fan of modern jazz, or indeed anything modern, singling out the three Ps – Picasso, Pound and Charlie Parker – for special condemnation. Larkin proceeded from the standpoint that, to be any good at all, jazz must remain in touch with its harmonic roots, the blues, and that it must swing – a line similar to the one that Wynton Marsalis would later spin. Larkin revealed his true feelings for the first time in the famous preface to his collected criticism, explaining that he had never wanted to spell it out in the criticism itself for fear that the records might stop arriving at his door. After all, this was 1961, the heyday of modern jazz; who would continue to employ a jazz critic who hated all the new stuff? Larkin's solution, therefore, was to praise everything to the skies. Yet while he might secretly have disliked Monk's music and Monk's '*faux-naif* elephant dance' on the keyboard, he wrote about both of them rather accurately – referring, for example, to Monk's 'gawky intervals'. 'Gawky' is surely the word.

A simpatico critic, Stanley Crouch, called Monk 'the first Picasso of jazz', and this, perhaps, is more germane (though it would have caused Larkin to raise an eyebrow). For as the twentieth century's most famous artist approached his ninetieth birthday, he began, quite suddenly, to paint like a child. It was not only that the application of paint had a childlike quality, or that, very often, his subjects, shapes and patterns seemed barely to fit on the canvas or paper, but also that his sheer productivity was that of an unstoppable pre-schooler. Between January 1969 and February 1970, Picasso finished – if that is the word – 167 new paintings, many of them quite large.

In the first full biography of Picasso following his death, the novelist Patrick O'Brian wrote of going to see these works in 1972 at Avignon in the Palace of the Popes. He was horrified. The paintings, he wrote, 'bore all the hallmarks of furious haste'. Complaining of 'coarse slashing brushstrokes', he noted that Picasso had simply 'flung' the paint at his canvases 'or in some cases on to the bare brown paper' and left it 'running down in streaks'. It was, O'Brian concluded, 'a deliberate denial of all technique'.

O'Brian went on to speculate that Picasso had been heeding Dylan Thomas's advice to his father to 'rage against the dying of the light', but perhaps there was more to it than this. Yes, the painter's sheer prolificacy might well have been explained by his snarling at death, staving off the end of his life with hyperactive brushstrokes. But when O'Brian accuses Picasso of denying technique, it may be that he misses the mark. Perhaps, like Monk, Picasso was employing a childlike technique in order to find a kind of truth in his work that would otherwise have been unavailable to him. And perhaps, for both Monk and Picasso, that truth was to do with confronting first and last things.

In painting, it is comparatively easy to recognise a childlike technique because we have all seen – indeed, we've all made – children's drawings; what is more, we know their power. When, in his *New York Times* obituary of Cy Twombly, Randy Kennedy wrote of the artist's 'spare, childlike scribbles', he was not being critical. That is how most of Twombly's mature work appears – studiedly immature.

In literature, the same approach is quite common, a child's language or writing style used to reveal something about childhood, or to reveal the world through a child's eyes. James Joyce's *A Portrait of the Artist as a Young Man* (1916) begins with a child's story told in baby-language, its rationale quickly revealed: our artist is in his crib. It takes longer to appreciate what is going on in the opening pages of William Faulkner's *The Sound and the Fury* (1929), because here the childlike voice is sustained for seventy-odd pages. In fact, this time it is not a child who is telling the tale, but the 'idiot' alluded to in the Shakespearian title, the slow-witted, thirty-three-year-old Benjy Compson. We won't find that out until another narrator takes over the story, but in the meantime we begin, bit by bit, to be able to follow Benjy's stream of consciousness, and we sense his particular brand of wisdom: while he may not understand the significance of the events he relates, he sees them very clearly indeed. 'They took the flag out, and they were hitting,' Benjy tells us. We work out, later, that he enjoys watching golf.

* * *

Musical depictions of childhood come in various forms, usually with a degree of simplicity or nostalgia (Schumann's *Kinderszenen*, for instance), and in popular music that is generally as far as it gets. But sometimes a degree of homespun awkwardness can inject a song with the essence of childhood or youth and, moreover, with a point of view. In the Go-Betweens' 'Cattle and Cane' (1983), for instance, the fluctuating metre of Grant McLennan's song (six beats alternating with five) coupled with Lindy Morrison's precise snare-drum quavers, creates the effect not only of running but of a child's running – a bit too fast and in danger of toppling forwards. It's the musical embodiment of 'a schoolboy coming home', and also of growing up, of the newness and strangeness of everything.

The same year as 'Cattle and Cane', Violent Femmes released their hymn to bemused adolescence, 'Blister in the Sun'. Like 'Cattle and Cane', it is a guitar, bass and drums song, and again the snare drum has an illustrative role. Brian Ritchie's bass plays what sounds like a nervous, sped-up, 2/4 version of the famous riff that runs through the Crystals' 'Then He Kissed Me' (though Ritchie's phrasing also resembles Oscar Pettiford's bass line on 'Blues in the Closet'), its course interrupted after three bars by the snare. Victor DeLorenzo plays two double strokes, on the off-beats of the fourth bar, the second of them taking us by surprise, because the bass had, in no time at all, established a strong second beat, and suddenly it's gone. The effect of the delay is a percussive stutter, the sound of tongue-tied teenagers through history.

Like 'Blister in the Sun', Tom Waits's childhood reminiscence 'Kentucky Avenue' (1978) is first-person and present-tense, but otherwise the two songs are a long way apart. Where the Femmes' song is petulant and cool, Waits's is full of childlike wonder and, ultimately, romantic. It has a symphonic quality in the way the melody goes on developing and extending itself as the song reaches its climax. Much of the imagery in the song pertains to Waits's own childhood, though it is not important that we know this. He really did live on Kentucky Avenue and really did have a boyhood friend who was confined to a wheelchair. The song does not tell us about this friend — it shows him. Like Benjy Compson telling us about the 'hitting', Waits gives us images, and it is up to us how or whether we interpret them. In among the plethora of names and characters on 'Kentucky Avenue', a nameless 'you' emerges; as the song builds, Waits sings of taking 'the spokes from your wheelchair and a magpie's wings' and attaching them 'to your shoulders and your feet', then cutting 'the braces off your legs' with a stolen hacksaw.

Romantic it might be, but 'Kentucky Avenue' is not sentimental; children never are. Keeping sentimentality at bay is partly a function of the singer's extraordinary voice — a rasping, gravelly boom of a thing, the voice of some Old Testament prophet — and partly a function of his very specific use of names and images, even when the images (like Benjy's narrative) may seem foreign to us. Apparently, young Tom believed that a freight train ran through the hallway in his family's home; knowing this explains a reference in the final verse, but it doesn't need explaining. In fact, it's all the more magical without that information.

Waits, this hipster Ezekiel, might have the wrong voice for the song – there's nothing childlike about the sound – but his manner of singing is correct. He tells us secrets in a confidential tone, and we hear an eye-rolling leer when he reports that Hilda put her tongue in Joey Naviski's mouth.

In utter contrast, Blossom Dearie's singing was fragile and fey; she had 'a childlike wisp of a voice', according to James Gavin in his book *Intimate Nights*, though it was often tinged with irony. In concert, even her speaking voice sounded this way as she introduced her songs. And yet unlike her name, which was real enough, the voice was a confection, something she had evolved over a lifetime of performing. On her early recordings she sounds stronger and altogether more womanly, like her normal speaking voice – unless she was in character for an interview. But up on stage in the last three decades of her long performing career, she became a child.

She brought new meaning to familiar standards such as 'If I Were a Bell' and 'I Won't Dance', making both songs into expressions of wide-eyed and slightly alarmed innocence, and she sought out new material that fitted this persona. 'I'm Hip', 'My Attorney Bernie', 'Someone Is Sending Me Flowers' (*sic*, Dearie changed the words) and 'Bruce' might have been written for her and her style of delivery. In fact, they weren't; she just made them brilliantly her own.

'I think Blossom went into a little room somewhere when she was a child and never came out,' the New York saloon pianist

Murray Gold told Gavin, and the remark might serve for any number of jazz and pop singers, female and male. From Cyndi Lauper at her poutiest ('Oh Daddy, dear, you know you're still number one, / But girls, they want to have fu-un') to Björk, especially in her days with the Sugarcubes, popular music has had a lot of cute, childlike voices.

A lot of cute children, too. In 1962, 'Little' Stevie Wonder, the '12 Year Old Genius', released his first record, and at sixteen (minus the 'Little') had his first hit. The prepubescent Michael Jackson fronted the Jackson 5 from 1964, when he was six years old, having four consecutive number-one records with the group at the age of eleven. And when fifteen-year-old Donny Osmond's voice changed, making him sound a bit too old to be the child at the front of the Osmonds, along came his nine-year-old brother, 'Little' Jimmy Osmond, to assume the mantle.

The public's appetite for child performers is nothing new. Occasionally it results in the destruction of the performer – one thinks of Lena Zavaroni – and it can seldom do them much good, but we like it when a child is confident and talented, and prodigies have been part of the culture for centuries – think of the boy Mozart touring Europe with his father. But with singers there's more to it, the child's voice seeming to carry a special kind of authority, a prelapsarian wisdom (like Benjy's). We thrill to the sound of a choir containing the voices of small boys or girls, even though the performance might lack some of the richness and nuance to be found in an equivalent performance by women and men. But it's more than just the sound.

In jazz, the androgynous voices of Chet Baker and 'Little' Jimmy Scott make an interesting comparison. In Scott's case, the gorgeous contralto was the result of Kallmann syndrome and a failure to complete puberty, and he used it with great power and effect. There was sometimes a touch of Shirley Bassey about his torch songs; listening to his recordings, you often forget that a man is singing. In contrast, Baker's waif-like high tenor sounded artless – not unlike his trumpet playing – and that was what gave it its power. Towards the end of his life, he toured Scandinavia with Stan Getz; the laid-back, heroin-addicted trumpeter and the angry-drunk saxophonist were ill-matched. Getz was irritated by Baker's singing, which he considered pallid and silly (he also hated the fact that women flocked to the trumpeter), and he ended up having Baker dismissed from the tour.

Baker's singing was certainly pallid, but never silly. His talent was to be minimal, placing his considerable technique at the service of a spare, pure style of playing and singing. When Baker sang 'My Funny Valentine' or 'I Get Along Without You Very Well', you heard the songs with great clarity; he revealed them simply yet starkly, as a child might. And when he played the trumpet, it was often what he left out that counted. There were no unnecessary notes in his performances; he could skate through a song, delicately pointing its melodic line, nudging its harmonic structure, accentuating a particular phrase. And his cracked notes were pure heartbreak, calculated imperfection part of his art.

* * *

The Western classical canon, vast and varied as it is, depends upon a notion of fidelity to the score. Acknowledging the role that interpretation and human frailty play in this, the great pianist Artur Schnabel once remarked that no performance of a Beethoven sonata could be as great as the sonata itself. Perhaps inevitably, then, over the last century or so, a sub-genre has developed in what we may still broadly call 'classical music' that permits and thrives upon notions of non-fidelity and even imperfection.

Percy Grainger's *Random Round* (1912–14) is an early 'mobile' score. An example of Grainger's 'elastic scoring', the piece sanctions a wide range of options for instrumentation, while the performers who take part may, as the title suggests, join in and drop out, almost at will. The score consists of a strongly rhythmic, chordal spine, played (Grainger suggests) on a 'gut-strung guitar', with short melodic lines that can be played in canon or woven together more or less at will. Grainger called the piece 'a join-in when-you-like Round', and something of the same spirit hovers over Terry Riley's *In C* (1964). This San Franciscan 'happening' of a piece, in which Riley animated the drones of La Monte Young and Pauline Oliveros, has a pulse as strong as Grainger's in *Random Round*. It also fits the 'join-in when-you-like' description. The attraction of *In C* was both its hypnotic high spirits and its homemade nature. For both Grainger and Riley, music was at its best when at its most inclusive.

Frederic Rzewski's *Les moutons de Panurge* (1969) is 'for any number of musicians playing melody instruments and any number of non-musicians playing anything'. The musicians, like the

sheep in the work's Rabelaisian title, all do the same thing, playing a fast (and accelerating), cumulative melodic line in unison,
until one or more of them comes unstuck. Rzewski (born 1938)
instructs any lost player (sheep) to stay lost ('Do not try to find
your way back to the fold'). The melodic material should be very
loud and amplified, and when the written notes run out, the
players may improvise. The non-musicians, meanwhile, have a
pulse to play, but the composer encourages civil disobedience
right from the start. There is a conductor who may be followed
or ignored; the motto of these players, the score advises, should
be: 'The left hand doesn't know what the right hand is doing.'
What the audience hears is a long melodic line which gradually
unravels, the music ending in a sort of ecstatic anarchy.

Rzewski himself was a virtuoso pianist who gave early performances of some of the most demanding works of the post-war
avant-garde (Boulez, Stockhausen et al.). But as a composer, and
a man of the political left, his attitude was more embracing. Even
those of his pieces that are properly in the domain of the virtuoso (for example, *The People United Will Never Be Defeated*,
an hour-long set of variations on a Chilean protest song to rival
Beethoven's *Diabelli* variations) have a political purpose or lesson,
but *Les moutons de Panurge*, which could be played by anyone at
all, was a key work for this composer.

In 1970 a group of fine-arts students at Portsmouth Polytechnic
in the south of England formed an orchestra, the Portsmouth Sinfonia, with a view to playing popular classics. What was noteworthy
about the enterprise was that the orchestra largely comprised

non-musicians. Skilled players were permitted in the ranks, but only if they performed on an instrument that was unfamiliar to them. What began as little more than a student prank quickly became something more interesting. The advantage of tackling well-known pieces – Tchaikovsky's *1812* overture, for example, and Rossini's overture to *William Tell* – was that even though the players could mostly not read their parts, they had at least a rough idea of how the music should go. Two future record producers were members of the Sinfonia, Arun Chakraverty and Brian Eno (who in fact produced the LP *Portsmouth Sinfonia Plays the Popular Classics* in 1974), but the orchestra's guiding light – if that's not too strong a term – was the composer Gavin Bryars (born 1943), who stipulated that the players must at least attempt to play the right notes. In other words, what one hears when listening to one of the Portsmouth Sinfonia's recordings is not the sound of students mucking about, but of non-musicians earnestly trying and, of course, failing to perform Tchaikovsky or Rossini. The end result, though cacophonous, was mostly recognisable, often comic and sometimes oddly touching.

Music played or sung by non-musicians was a feature of the work of another English composer of this time, Cornelius Cardew (1936–81), whose pieces were increasingly guided by his political beliefs. At his most experimental, he co-founded a performing group named the Scratch Orchestra, for which he composed a number of works based on the *Analects of Confucius*. Collectively known as *The Great Learning*, there are seven pieces or 'paragraphs', the last of which, entirely vocal, is an exercise in musical democracy for a large number of singers.

The score of 'Paragraph 7' provides the singers with a short passage from Confucius, divided into twenty-five lines, each containing one, two or three words. Each line is sung a specified number of times, each time for the duration of a single breath. Since the individual singers' lung capacities will differ, it follows that each singer will move through the piece at a different rate. Most of the singing is quiet, but certain lines are marked to be sung loudly (once or twice), resulting in little solos emerging from the mass of voices. At the start of the piece, the singers are grouped together, but each may choose his or her own starting note. A gentle, random and usually very dense cloud of sound ensues. The singers hold their notes as best they can until the end of their first line (remember, each singer will arrive at this point individually), but then adopts the pitch of another singer who is nearby or who happens to be singing loudly at the time. This process continues, so that over the course of fifteen or twenty minutes the range of pitches narrows from the original tone cluster to a unison (often enough), or an open fifth or some other rather simple interval.

In the early twenty-first century, three Australian musicians – the composers and visual artists Julian Day (born 1975) and Luke Jaaniste (born 1977), and the flute player Janet McKay (born 1973) – worked on a series of performances under the broad title *Super Critical Mass* (2007–). Some of the performances were for instruments – particularly choirs of similar instruments, a hundred flutes, say – and some for voices. In all cases the performances involved elements of individual freedom and group cooperation. The artists' debt to Cardew's 'Paragraph 7' was clear, but they took his ideas further. For one thing, place was important – massed brass players surrounding the lake in New York's Central Park, massed singers filling Manchester Cathedral – and so was collaboration. The artists of *Super Critical Mass* did not take a score, however imprecise, to their first rehearsal; they planned the piece first by taking the soundings of the performance space, and then worked out the details by sounding out the performers. In a sense, Day, Jaaniste and McKay were convenors and leaders as much as composers.

In June 2014, Sydney's Museum of Contemporary Art was the site for a *Super Critical Mass* performance in which, to quote Day, 'kids, seniors, choristers, artists, office workers, driving instructors' came together to sing on the museum's second floor during public opening hours. Some art lovers knew there would be a performance, and some did not. The seventy-five singers, dressed as casually as the punters, might have been there to see the artworks too. Threaded through various rooms of different size housing part of the MCA's permanent collection, the singers gave an hour-long performance of considerable subtlety. Depending upon their position on the floor, participants might sing short solos or, finding themselves in a small group with other singers, tune into the surrounding voices. Much of the time there was little more than an ambient hum as evidence that a performance was taking place, but a couple of times during the hour the whole mass of singers clustered together to sing as one.

The fact that a driving instructor may participate in a performance at a prestigious cultural centre – and not simply as a singer, but as a singer who makes choices about when and how to sing, and who is helping devise the structure of the overall work – says a lot about *Super Critical Mass*. It is, evidently, a project concerned with social access, demystification of the creative act and democracy. But if it did not also sound good, there would be no musical point to it. Day, Jaaniste and McKay are particularly interested in exploring multiple versions of the same basic sound. One hundred flutes playing together also form a single super flute. The resultant music is partly an exploration of the essence of the instruments or voices involved.

The prospect of finding a hundred professional flute players (let alone paying them) or two thousand trained singers would have derailed *Super Critical Mass* before it got started, so there is a purely pragmatic side to designing the project with amateurs, non-musicians and driving instructors in mind. But there is also a sonic advantage. Just as a film director such as Pier Paolo Pasolini liked to work with non-actors because they do less on screen, so in *Super Critical Mass* the non-professionals are likely to be blanker, better able to blend, and – because their performance depends upon it – possibly better at listening.

Of course, the artists behind *Super Critical Mass* are anything but non-musicians. At the 'classical' end of music, it is hard to find works that are genuinely primitive. Projects as musically ambitious and carefully planned as *Super Critical Mass* are unlikely to come from the musically untrained, and that is before notation comes into it. A classical composer can try to be primitive, and can certainly bring in primitive sounds and sources and techniques, but when it comes to notation that can be read and played from, a degree of sophistication is necessary. Also, composing with notation is a reflective process; it cannot yield instant sound.

But with new recording and composing technologies – ever simpler, ever cheaper – that is beginning to change. If the music is to be interesting, the creator must have talent (or a considerable amount of luck), but a sophisticated grasp of instrumental capacities and notational gambits may no longer be a necessary precursor. If you type in a note that a piccolo can't play, the computer will tell you. It's possible for talented children to have orchestras in their bedrooms, obeying their every whim and command. Anyway, who says you need an orchestra?

Among singer–songwriters, the ability to make up words and a tune, to master a few guitar chords and to record your efforts on basic equipment is commonplace: it's how most of them start. Even so, Daniel Johnston is an extreme example. Johnston was born in Sacramento, California, in 1961, and his earliest recordings date from his teenage years. In fact he could play the piano rather well, but he recorded the songs himself on a mono boom box in his basement. The quality of the demos was as lo-fi as you might imagine, and the quality of the songs variable, but he found a following by passing out cassette tapes of his music to passers-by in the street.

Johnston was diagnosed with a bipolar disorder fairly early on, and some of his fame and much of his critical acclaim rests on that, as though his childlike voice, basic gift for a catchy tune and lyrical obsession with redemptive love were the result of mental illness. Apart from the fact that he shared the voice, melodic gift and lyrical obsession with hundreds of other better-recorded singer–songwriters, it is also true that history is full of high-functioning mentally ill creative artists; in this regard, Johnston is not so very special. His pleas for help on a song such as 'Peek a Boo' (1982) doubtless fuelled his popular image as an outsider, but equally he could also turn accusingly on his fans, as he did in 'Like a Monkey in a Zoo' (1981).

The real power of Johnston's art lies in its homespun quality. On 'True Love Will Find You in the End' (1990), his guitar is out of tune and his voice is not quite in sync with it. But the singing is strong and hopeful and ardent, and the apparently spontaneous repetition in the line 'step out into the light, the light' curiously touching. The performance is live, real, raw and simple, and its recorded sound is undeniably primitive. But it is also compelling. Once you begin listening to Daniel Johnston, it is hard to stop.

12

Looking for Momentum

AN INTERVIEW WITH BRIAN ENO

Brian Eno (born in Woodbridge, Suffolk, in 1948) is a composer, key-board player, record producer and, by common assent, the inventor of ambient music. A member of Roxy Music in the early 1970s, he went on to produce David Bowie's Berlin albums as well as albums for Talking Heads, U2, Paul Simon, Laurie Anderson, Sinéad O'Connor and many others. We recorded this interview for The Music Show *in Sydney in 2009, when Eno was artistic director of the Vivid festival. It has been edited for this book.*

ANDREW FORD: I was very struck by something I heard you say on the telly the other day – on the news, actually – about how you were into seduction. You said that you weren't interested in the idea of art being some sort of existential challenge, that you wanted to do something irresistible. Maybe that's a place to begin, with the idea that art is something which seduces you.

BRIAN ENO: Yes, I think that until the twentieth century, that was completely taken for granted, that art had to be something that was irresistible, that overwhelmed you, that you felt, Oh my gosh, I've got to stop and listen to this! It was only in the twentieth century that the idea came up that the middle classes needed to be shaken out of their torpor, and the way to do it was by smacking people around the face with kippers. And okay, that has its place, it's just not what I want to do.

AF: Right. But Beethoven's fifth symphony doesn't really seduce you, does it? It comes and grabs you by the throat.

BE: Well, it's very grand, but yes, I think it does seduce you. It says, 'Here I am, I'm big, I'm powerful and I'm beautiful. Better pay attention.' You know, if you like it at all, you like it because you surrender to it, and it offers you a chance to just stop being you in your little life, and suddenly you're part of a huge big thing. You feel you are, anyway.

AF: I promise I'm not just going to throw quotes at you, but there is another one which goes back quite a lot further. It's 1978 actually, in David Toop's book *Ocean of Sound*, and he quotes you, saying that you believe we're moving towards a position of using music and recorded sound with a variety of options as we presently use colour to tint the environment. This sounds pretty seductive too, actually. And I wonder whether this is an idea which has lasted in your work, the idea of creating an environment or perfuming an environment.

BE: Funny you should use the word 'perfume', because that's also something I'm interested in, working with smells. As I often say to people, I think that there really ought to be a different name for all the stuff that happened since recording. You know, we still call it 'music', but we don't still call cinema 'filmed theatre' or something like that. We realise that there's a difference between live theatre and films. Cinema has all sorts of possibilities and all sorts of conventions that are quite different from theatre, and in fact are impossible in theatre. There's a similar relationship, I think, between performed music and recorded music. Recorded music is something completely different, and really deserves a different name, and then a lot of confusion would disappear if that were the case, if you just sort of accepted that it doesn't really have to have much to do with performance.

So one of the things I realised in the early 1970s, with a lot of other people, was that I was using music in a different way from how music had been used before recording, which is to say I was using it as part of my landscape. The thing about a record is that you put it on when and where you want it, you adjust the volume, you fit it into your world. It's the opposite of going to a concert hall, actually, where you fit into its world. You completely submit to the terms and conditions, and in fact you're told to shut up, and only cough between movements and so on. You're completely controlled by the music, by the situation of the music. [With recorded music,] you create the situation, and you use the music as a way of doing that.

So I became aware that music was part of people's lifestyle, and of course composers weren't working at the time for that idea. If you bought an album, you'd have a fast track, then a slow track, then a sad track, then a happy track, et cetera, et cetera, and the whole idea was variety. Well, if you're trying to create a space, you don't want variety, you want the opposite, you want consistency, you want something that you can make part of that space reliably, just like you would with light, you know, if you're trying to light your flat, you don't want the light to constantly be changing colour and going on and off. Well, you might do, but that's an advanced usage, that's a choice you want to be able to make.

AF: But you make it sound a bit like interior decorating, and it's not that, is it? I mean, it's not just creating an ambience, it's more than that – you're inviting people in with your work. So in fact, you've got a foot in each camp, because on the one hand you're doing seduction in confronting people with the music – in making some demands on them, you are being like a classical composer in the concert hall – and then you're also saying, 'But you can use this yourself, you can tailor it to your own needs.' So it's a bit of both.

BE: Yes, I think it is a bit of both. So I certainly didn't start out on the ambient path with the idea I was inventing a totally new music, or destroying old music or anything like that. I was really, I felt, responding to the way in which people were listening to music then. I think ambient is more about how you listen than what you make as a composer. And it started really with a particular incident.

I was in an airport in Cologne, a beautiful airport, lovely architecture and everything very well designed, and it was a lovely Sunday morning, with the sun streaming in through the windows. And I thought: Wow, this is great, this is modern life, this is what it feels like to live in the twentieth century. Except that there was a crummy cassette playing terrible music over the PA, some German pop music, and I thought it's ridiculous that this aspect of the design of the place hasn't been considered. They've spent so much money on the architecture and the interior design, and every aspect of the visual side of the airport, [but] the sonic side has been left to whoever happened to bring in a cassette that day. And I thought it's ridiculous that composers aren't addressing this type of issue. We know this is what people are doing with music now; why not give them the right music to do it with? Why not give them something that's designed with the same sort of sense of scale and space that the architecture is?

So that's what gave rise to *Music for Airports* [1978]. And that was deliberately a response to two things: one, people are listening to music in a different way, and there ought to be music to satisfy that kind of listening; and secondly, we are now in a new technological environment where there are speakers everywhere. There are PA systems, people are going to be playing music in big open spaces like that; what's the right music for that?

AF: One of the things that is quite striking about *Music for Airports* is that the listener is in control. You can ignore it – I mean, I suppose most of the time at airports, the music is ignored, whatever it is. But you could also focus on it, and if we use the same example of Beethoven's fifth symphony, that's a very hard piece to ignore. You can't really shut it out. You can switch it off, but it's pretty hard to have a conversation with Beethoven's fifth going on in the background, so there is a difference, isn't there?

BE: Yes, that's an important difference, and one of the reasons for that difference is because the Beethoven piece is kind of narrative, in the sense that it has development. It has a beginning, a statement of themes, an argument, an investigation of those themes, and a climax and an ending. So it's a story, really, in some sense. So that of course doesn't work in the kind of listening situation in the airport. People don't have time to sit and listen to a whole story, and they've got other things to do: they've got to get on a plane and listen to announcements, and there are going to be announcements. So I was thinking: What can you make that can be interrupted? What can you make that can be at the edge of people's consciousness and not disturb them if they have something to do, but which is also nice enough so that if they do want to listen, it's there and they can have a proper experience with it? It's not some cheap thing experienced like muzak was. So I thought for a composer this was a very interesting set of demands. And that's what I want to address.

But you're right, the main issue for me, as I said on the cover notes of that record, was to make something that was as ignorable as it is interesting. So now we find this odd in music, because we're used to the idea of music being at the foreground of our attention; we don't find it odd with paintings. If you have a painting on the wall, you don't feel that you've done the painting a disservice by turning away [and] looking at the television, or having a conversation with your friend. A painting is always there – sometimes you pay attention to it, a lot of the time you don't. So I was sort of thinking of a music that moved towards the position in our lives, like paintings, of being there when we wanted it, and being ignorable when we didn't want it.

AF: So you need to keep doing the same thing pretty much, then, don't you?

BE: Exactly.

AF: Because otherwise you'll miss something important.

BE: Yes, that's exactly right. So you want something that is fairly steady-state. Of course, since it moves in time, there will be variation – in fact, the *Music for Airports*, and the ambient experiments, led on to what I call generative music, which is a construction of machines and systems that constantly generate changing music. But it doesn't change much; it changes in the same way that a river changes, where it's the same river but it's always a little bit different from moment to moment. So this was my intention, to make a sort of organic communalism of some kind.

AF: I suppose the quality of the sound that you create is as important really, in this music, as the content.

BE: In fact, in my case I think it's more important. That really is the issue. It's like some painters are obsessed with colour. Colour is the thing in the work of one of your best Australian painters, Sidney Nolan; I would say he is one whose real interest was in colour, so he used form as a carrier for what he wanted to do with colour. I would say I'm rather like that musically as well. I do use form, obviously – there's no choice – but it's there really as a carrier for sonic texture.

And one of the other things that people don't realise about recording and electronics is that the effect on composers has been to suddenly broaden the palette incredibly. It's a little bit like if you went up to a painter and said, 'Okay, you've got these seven basic spectrum colours you've been used to using, here's another four thousand.' That's about the scale of expansion that we've had. You know, if you think of classical instruments, let's say, there is the clarinet, there is the violin, there is the grand piano, the oboe, and each one of those words describes a little sort of island of possible sounds, which of course people became very good at exploiting and understood very well. But nonetheless there was [a limit] to what an oboe was and what it could do. If you say 'synthesiser', it doesn't describe anything, except a huge, huge, ever-expanding landscape of sound: it's not an island at all, it's a universe of sounds. And even an electric guitar is like that, perhaps . . . even the *voice* now is becoming like that, as we find new ways of processing voices. So we're now in a world where the palette is absolutely enormous, and increasing every day; literally every day somebody's coming up with new technologies to do things, song included, we couldn't do before.

AF: I first encountered the name Brian Eno on those gorgeous green-tinted, Obscure LPs that came out in, I suppose, the mid 1970s. They contained such a lot of very interesting music, much of it rather prescient on your part, because some of these composers who one had never heard of at the time have become quite big names – like Gavin Bryars, for example.

BE: John Adams, Michael Nyman. Yes, they made their first albums there.

AF: Maybe we could do a bit of history and talk about not just the Obscure record label but the whole area that you came from, that was part of your own musical education and that, I suppose, helped to form your ideas: experimental music in general, and in particular a rather quirky English style of experimentalism.

BE: Well, it all came out of the 1960s. And the 1960s, of course, all came out of the 1950s. But in the '60s in England there was a very exciting scene. It was quite small, but it was very lively indeed. There was a real crossover between art schools and experimental music. In fact, one of the only places that experimental composers like Cornelius Cardew and Christian Wolff and Tom Phillips and so on could find a job was in art schools. Music schools wanted

absolutely nothing to do with them, so art schools took those people in and said, 'Oh, we think there's a kind of overlap between
what you're doing and what we're doing.'

Cardew was a very important figure. He created the Scratch
Orchestra, which I belonged to, and which was mostly art students. I think there were about eighty of us in it at the peak, and
it was very, very experimental. There were extremely strange scores,
[consisting] of directions for how to make pieces of music that
really were nothing like conventional music scores. They didn't
have any notation, for instance, they would have a description of
something, some action that we should do: 'Cover a surface in
pencil,' or something like that. And we said, 'What does that mean?
How does that make music?' So each one was a sort of riddle or a
problem, and it kind of created a way of thinking that I think did
energise English music, off into a different direction, because there
were two very strong international schools going on at that time.
There was the European one, with Stockhausen and Boulez, people like that, which looked very much like a sort of logical extension of twentieth-century avant-garde music. You could sort of
trace the lineage through Schoenberg and Hindemith and see how
that turned into Stockhausen, Boulez.

AF: And back to Beethoven, for that matter.

BE: Yes, yes, that's right. So it was very much part of a story that
had been going on for a few hundred years. But then suddenly there
appeared this very interesting group of American composers –

Terry Riley, Steve Reich, Philip Glass, John Gibson, a few other people – who were suddenly doing something that sidestepped that narrative, and were using very simple chords that we could all understand, and simple tonalities, and doing a huge amount of repetition, which of course was anathema to Stockhausen, who hated the idea of people repeating themselves. And that suddenly sounded fresh to me.

And so we in England were sort of straddled between those two, and I have to say we took more from Cage and from the Americans than from the Europeans. But nonetheless, it was something different from both of them. And to me, it was really exciting and original, and so I knew about this scene and I knew who was involved, and it amazed me that there were no records of it, nobody was releasing records. And I kind of naively thought, God, if you put this on record, everybody would want to buy it – it's so interesting! Well, that turned out not to be true, but in fact you're quite right, that several of the people who were on those first ten albums ended up being important figures.

AF: And the Penguin Café Orchestra. And suddenly we're taking a step into pop music, really, aren't we? I mean, they were maybe one part pop to two parts experimental, or whatever you want to call it. We should talk about that as well, because some of your major collaborations have been with the likes of Roxy Music (of course) and Bowie, U2, Paul Simon and David Byrne. I'm interested in the way in which you collaborate. When you walk into a studio with somebody who's trying to make a pop record, what do you do?

BE: I'm always excited by strangeness, shall we say, or unfamiliarity. So I think that's the first important difference from other producers, because I think what normally happens when people go into a studio – not always, of course; there are a lot of great producers around – but what can happen is that the producer gets very excited when he hears more of the same. You know: 'Oh, that's like that big hit you had three years ago – let's do more of that.' I'm not that excited when I hear that. I can appreciate that people like to have hits and so on, but I don't want to be remaking things; in fact, I'm not very good at remaking things – I don't know how you do it.

So I get excited when I hear something and I think: Wow, that's a new feeling – I've never had that mixture of feelings before. And I tend to jump on those things and encourage them. Artists tell me that this is actually what they like, this is unusual for them, because what often happens is that they've got some kind of clumsy new idea, they're not at all sure about it, they don't know how to do it and it doesn't get very much encouragement. It's much easier to encourage something else that you know the destination of. So I'm always madly enthusiastic about the newer sides of someone's work, and I think people like that, because that's where they want to be going. And of course the newer things are always very awkward – they're like newborn babies: they all look like tomatoes, and you can only love them if they're your own, really.

AF: So you help to give them personality, do you? You help in their education, these newborn babies?

BE: I think encouragement is very important, and I think people thrive on encouragement, and they also thrive on strong opinions. It's really thrilling to have somebody around who'll say, 'Oh, it's the worst trash I've ever heard,' or 'I'm in heaven; play more of that.' It's so much more useful than having somebody around who kind of says, 'Oh, that's quite good,' you know. That doesn't really contribute anything to the situation; you want to put energy into a situation, you want it to come to life. [Sometimes that] means having a really good argument about something – not a bad-natured argument but, you know, forcing someone to stand their ground: 'If you think this is good, show me why; I don't believe it. Show me what it could be.' It makes people think: Okay, I bloody well will. I'll show him!

AF: I believe you like to work fast. I'm interested in this. Obviously it makes things more efficient if you can push ahead. But are you looking for energy or spontaneity?

BE: I think I'm looking for momentum. And I think momentum can get dissipated very easily if you decide to explore all the options; there are too many options. You end up sort of doing a secretarial job of ticking off: you could do that; no, it's not working; that's quite nice; you could do that. I just don't like that feeling when the work in the studio settles down to a sort of comfortable bureaucracy. I like it when people are thrilled, because what comes through in music more than anything else is how thrilled people are, how alive they are when they're doing it. It doesn't matter where the bloody microphones are standing or if we haven't properly miked up the bass drum, all that sort of thing; it's not irrelevant, but it's so far down on the scale of relevance compared to 'Have we captured some life in this thing?' And life can take all sorts of forms – it can be energy, it can be the sense of intellectual passion, it can be the sense of someone absolutely enjoying surrendering to a feeling that they're having at the time. Whatever it is, that's what communicates to listeners, I think, and that's what we producers and artists should be trying to capture. And so when I'm working, I'm always trying very hard to make sure that we retain that priority, that we're trying to capture that feeling of discovery: Ah, listen to this, this is amazing! Because that's what I want the listeners to be thinking, and they're not likely to if we weren't.

AF: And this extends to lyric writing as well? You like first thoughts, don't you?

BE: Yes, well, I think it's because of the way people write lyrics. Now, I think, most people imagine that songwriters come in with a sort of set of verses and choruses all nicely written and rhymed up, and then they sit down and write some chords around them, and it becomes a song. Well, there are a few people who work like that. I think Bob Dylan does, and a few others. But most people don't write songs that way. What they do is, they come up with a musical idea which they like, and they're playing it, and the start [sings . . .] – you know, they sing nonsense, basically, but that nonsense is musically appropriate, rhythmically appropriate.

It fits. It's what they want to be doing with their voice. Now, what often happens is that they think, I'm a lyric writer – I'd better be saying something serious, so they then painstakingly change that all into words, and it sounds incredibly clumsy; it just doesn't flow, it doesn't run.

AF: Because they're going for meaning as opposed to sound.

BE: Yes, that's right, and rock critics focus on lyrics because it's the language that they're used to. It's easy to write about lyrics and hard to write about music. So it makes songwriters think: Oh, I'd better get my lyrics up to scratch; I'd better be saying something. I don't give a screw about what people are saying generally; I think if you're really talking about saying something, then making something that works musically says a great deal. That's the message I want to give. It doesn't mean that I want them to write bad lyrics, but my criterion is [that they] write lyrics which support the music.

13

Earth Dances

Earth feet, loam feet . . .

T.S. Eliot, 'East Coker', *Four Quartets*

It is as though the ground is opening, the earth's crust breaking apart. The hollow noise comes from nowhere, building to a roar; then it dies away – droops, rather – leaving a void, a sense of loss and of foreboding. And then, suddenly, it is back again. The same roar: two contrabassoons, four trombones, two tubas, pairs of bass drums and tam-tams, nine cellos and nine double basses, all in a horrifying groundswell of sound, reinforced by a piano at the very bottom of its range, the player instructed to play *martellato brutale* – like a brutal hammer.

This is the start of Harrison Birtwistle's *Earth Dances* (1986), a tense, volatile work for large orchestra that, throughout its thirty-eight minutes, never loosens its hold on the listener's emotions. When the piece is not pulsing and jigging alarmingly, violently, the music tends to brood, dissolving into long, slow, unpredictable melodic lines that themselves seem likely to erupt into further violence.

For Birtwistle and his audience, *Earth Dances* was a midlife summing up of the composer's musical concerns to date, a compendium of devices and habits shaped into something like an epic. At its first performance, in London on 14 March 1986, it was greeted as a masterpiece, and more than one commentator compared it to *The Rite of Spring*. It was a comparison the piece itself invited, its very title invoking the 'Dance of the Earth' that concludes Part One of *The Rite*, while in its studied savagery Birtwistle's music might almost have been a homage to the Russian composer's seventy-three-year-old score. Even those opening sounds summoned memories of Stravinsky's comment about cracking ice. But there was something else as well, for in making reference to *The Rite of Spring*, Birtwistle also underlined the fact that each of his own musical works was at some level a 'rite'.

A rite or ritual involves the repetition, in a certain order, of certain actions – often in a certain (sacred) place. If you consider concert halls sacred places, then any musical performance there is a ritual, but Birtwistle's music suggests something deeper, older and more primitive, something of the earth. Like most rituals we see or hear, it is impossible for the uninitiated to comprehend exactly what is going on. In this case, Birtwistle is the only initiate, and it is a moot point how much even he is aware of the significance of his musical actions. But as a visit to a temple in a foreign land will often demonstrate, you do not have to know what is going on to feel the power of a ritual. That is certainly the case with Birtwistle's music.

Birtwistle's operas and music-theatre pieces all involve the ritualistic repetition of stories or elements of stories, and most draw on ancient or, at least, very old stories and story forms. In his first opera, *Punch and Judy* (1966–67), to a libretto by Stephen Pruslin, there is a series of ritual killings alongside a series of riddle games, and the whole thing has the formal structure of a Greek drama. *Down by the Greenwood Side* (1969), using a text by Michael Nyman, is designated a 'dramatic pastoral' and employs two interlocking structures of somewhat lesser antiquity. The first of these is the ballad 'The Cruel Mother', with its *Medea*-like story of infanticide and the refrain 'Down by the Greenwood Side'. The other is the traditional English mummers' play – a winter pageant that looks forward to the renewal of spring – in which St George is twice killed by the Saracen infidel Bold Slasher and twice revived, first by a doctor and then by a Green Man figure called Jack Finney; the master of ceremonies is Father Christmas. In *Bow Down* (1977), a collaboration between the composer, the poet Tony Harrison and actors of the National Theatre of Great Britain, another ballad, 'The Two Sisters', is spoken, chanted and sung over and over, in multiple versions from Scandinavia, Scotland and the north of England. This forms a foreground layer that intersects at key moments with a long, slow miming out of the general story. Similar devices are at play on a much grander scale in the operas *The Mask of Orpheus* (1973–84), *Gawain* (1990) and *The Minotaur* (2008), the recycling of certain narrative elements lending them a cool abstraction, even as the stories themselves deal in heightened emotions and, often enough, blood.

But even the composer's purely instrumental works are ritualistic at some level. It might be audible in the instrumental roleplay in the music: in Birtwistle's orchestral piece *The Triumph of*

Time (1972), two recurrent elements are a wandering, desolate cor anglais theme – never quite the same on each appearance, but instantly recognisable – and a slowly arching three-note figure (a rising major third followed by a falling perfect fourth) played by an amplified soprano saxophone. Both themes retain, to the end of the piece, their inscrutability, turning up like found objects amid the music's slow progress.

Another aspect of ritual and role-play in Birtwistle's music relates to how the players are seated in performance. In *Tragœdia* (1965), for example, a string quartet is situated on one side of the stage, cut off from a wind quintet on the other side by a centrally placed harp, so the audience is alerted to a ritual element before hearing a note of the music. In fact, this purely instrumental piece, as confronting in its impact today as when it was first performed, also makes thoroughgoing use of the structure of Greek tragedy, cutting abruptly – one might say remorselessly – from 'Parados' to 'Episodian', from 'Antistrophe' to 'Stasimon'.

Verses for Ensembles (1969), which also took its structure from Greek theatre, upped the ante in terms of unconventional seating arrangements with its terraced rows of wind, brass and percussion players. In fact, 'seating arrangement' does not really cover it, because in this piece the players actually move. The five woodwind players each play two instruments, high and low (piccolo and flute, clarinet and bass clarinet, bassoon and contrabassoon, etc.), sitting stage right to play the high instruments before moving to stage left to play the low. The percussionists play drums and other unpitched instruments from a platform raised up behind the brass players, but climb to a higher level still in order to play their tuned glockenspiels and xylophones. In addition, there are four stations at the corners of the performing area, to which individual players must walk in order to become temporary soloists.

The dramatic nature of the music – some of the most rebarbative that Birtwistle (or anyone else) has composed – encourages the listener to search for some extra-musical 'meaning'. But it is important to remember that there is no program behind it – at least, nothing the composer has ever owned up to – and no reason for the shape and sound of the music, save the purely musical logic of its composer's imagination.

After *Verses for Ensembles*, Birtwistle often asked his players to leave their seats mid-piece and move to a new playing position. Usually, this involved the player in question becoming the focal point of the music for a short time, playing a solo characterised by a new sort of music, suddenly lyrical or suddenly stentorian, perhaps using intervals that had hitherto not been associated with the instrument in question. One of the composer's most vivid exploitations of movement came in *Ritual Fragment* (1990), later reworked as *Cortège* (2007), composed for the London Sinfonietta in memory of its first artistic director, Michael Vyner. This piece – in both versions – arranges its fourteen players symmetrically; ten of them are required to move, in turn, to a central position near a bass drum, from which they declaim a solo. The evocation of a funeral ceremony is plain enough, a succession of mourners taking it in turns to step forward to recall the deceased, but typically Birtwistle's musical rituals were more impenetrable than this. One of the composer's key works from the 1980s, composed just prior to *Earth Dances*, was *Secret Theatre* (1986); as the title suggests, we have no idea why a player suddenly stands and moves to another part of the stage. The music of *Secret Theatre* is extremely compelling, but the rationale behind the sound and look of it will always elude us.

In 2013 Birtwistle explained to the writer Fiona Maddocks that he began each piece wholly from scratch; from his perspective, each work inhabited its own world. As a listener, it is hard to concur. Among the trademark techniques and textures that one associates with Birtwistle's music are the deep, dark sounds that begin *Earth Dances*. Like the cyclic forms and the ritual, these sounds have been typical of Birtwistle's larger-scale scores since the 1960s. All his orchestral works contain sections that plumb the sonic depths: the granite-textured brass-band piece *Grimethorpe Aria* (1973) explores this terrain in detail; *Gawain* is surely unique among operas in boasting a bottom-heavy orchestra that includes nine double basses, three tubas and a euphonium. Equally, the growling, snarling brass of *Earth Dances* was a feature of his work from *Nomos* (1965) and *Verses for Ensembles*, and all his subsequent music for orchestra or large ensemble. The cyclic, rhythmic structures that typify *Earth Dances* – clacking pulses that overlap and combine to create some demoniac clockwork – were certainly in evidence in *Tragœdia* (towards the end of this piece, four of the wind players exchange their instruments for wooden claves), while long, slow melodic lines have always been present in Birtwistle's music. You can hear them prominently, for example, in the gentle wailing of antiphonally placed sopranos in *The Fields of Sorrow* (1972) or the lamenting cor anglais of *The Triumph of Time* (1971–72).

If one wished to find a single early source for Birtwistle's musical obsessions, *Punch and Judy* might be the place to look. It was commissioned by the Aldeburgh Festival and received its world premiere there in 1968. Gossip had it that the festival's directors, Benjamin Britten and Peter Pears, fled the performance at interval, and this has tended to focus all subsequent attention on the nastiness of the work. As anyone who has seen a Punch and Judy puppet show will know, the anti-hero, Punch, is a conniving and bloodthirsty fellow whose irrepressible high spirits and victorious gloating ('*That's* the way to do it!') inveigles his young audience into supporting him in a succession of murderous acts, a typical show ending with a body count approaching that of *Hamlet*. But the nature of the violence in one of these shows is of the cartoon variety: Punch is very much a naughty boy rather than the murderous psychopath he would be in real life. With *Tragoedia*, Birtwistle had reminded his audience that the Greek word for tragedy literally means 'goat dance'. By much the same token, Birtwistle and Pruslin subtitled *Punch and Judy* 'a tragical comedy or a comical tragedy'.

Despite such equivocation, the issue of violence in Birtwistle's *Punch and Judy* and in his work in general remains tricky to discuss, not least because in interviews Birtwistle has tended to deny that his work deals in violence at all. But one cannot simply brush aside the murders in *Punch and Judy* (beginning with Punch's breaking of his baby's back before throwing it on a fire), Orpheus's dismemberment by the followers of Dionysus in *The Mask of Orpheus*, the dissection of a dead woman's genitalia in *Bow Down*, the beheading of the Green Knight in *Gawain* and the bloody orgy of killing in *The Minotaur*. All these libretti, while not by the composer himself, were in response to Birtwistle's initial ideas, so what does he intend by his theatre works if not meditations on violence?

Punch and Judy provides the key. Punch's gratuitous killing of his baby is part of the traditional show. Asked, by Judy, to look after their child, Punch proves himself inept, in some versions of the show accidentally feeding the infant into a sausage machine; the broken back and incineration seem to have been Pruslin's inventions. Yet, traditional though it may be, this part of the opera had a contemporary counterpart in Edward Bond's play *Saved* (1965), a *cause célèbre* of British theatre in which a group of youths stone to death a baby in its pram. The controversy over the play was still fresh at the time of the opera's first performance.

Cruelty and violence have always been part of theatre and of art. From the ancient Greeks to Shakespeare to Sarah Kane, plays have long confronted audiences with images of maiming, murder and all manner of mental and physical cruelty. The paintings of Francisco Goya – particularly those painted during and after the Peninsular War (1807–14) – depict the sufferings of war, imprisonment and torture, and much of his late work seems to be the product of mental illness. Folk ballads describe hideous cruelty. But when Birtwistle protests that he is not concerned with violence in his work, he is not being disingenuous.

The difference, for example, between the baby killings in *Saved* and *Punch and Judy* could hardly be greater. Bond, primarily a political playwright, came of age among the 'kitchen-sink' dramatists of the late 1950s an early 1960s, and while some of his early work also drew on surrealism and the epic theatre of Brecht, *Saved* is essentially naturalistic theatre in the service of political commentary. Above all, Bond is making a moral point, as his Shavian preface to the published play makes clear. He writes that 'if we are to improve people's behaviour we must first increase their moral understanding', and he seems to regard *Saved* as a mirror held up to society.

This is all a long way from Birtwistle, who is certainly not out to improve our behaviour. There is nothing naturalistic about this composer's operas – or about opera in general, you might say – and the fact that they are based on ancient mythology, mediaeval poetry and a children's seaside entertainment with its roots in *commedia dell'arte* only underlines their artificiality. In Birtwistle's opera, Punch's victims gradually assemble to form a chorus that comments on the action and finally accuses him; in *Gawain*, the Green Knight's decapitated head goes on singing, just as Orpheus's had done in *The Mask of Orpheus*; and throughout each of these works, the ritualised repetition of events distances us from the action and reminds us that we are hearing, seeing and exploring a labyrinthine structure, given its shape by big, even outlandish, events. As Birtwistle reminded Michael Hall in an interview, the painter Francis Bacon claimed that he had painted the Crucifixion so frequently because it was a big, formal subject, not for its religious meaning.

The Birtwistle/Bacon comparison is tempting for a number of reasons. One is that they were contemporaries who didn't really fit the mainstream, another that Bacon was also popularly supposed to deal in violence and also denied it. And then there was a connection through the art critic David Sylvester, a close friend of Birtwistle's who published a book-length interview with Bacon, *The Brutality of Fact*. Birtwistle referred Hall to the book, telling him that Bacon's views on the role of chance in his work matched the composer's own views. Bacon says, at one point, that much of his painting is to do with 'disrupting what I can do with ease', and implies that 'so-called chance' and 'accidents' assist him with this. Birtwistle spoke to Hall of 'a logic that's been disturbed' and 'a continuity that's been fractured'.

On the one hand, then, ritualised repetition; on the other, disruption – a broken ritual. This is the core of the 'violence' in Birtwistle's music – order is first established, then broken – and so it should not surprise us that, when writing music for the stage, this composer seeks out stories that dramatise his music. That is what the best composers do. And yet, paradoxically, the on-stage comic nastiness in *Punch and Judy* also tends to distract us from other features of the score, such as its lyricism. The love music between Punch and his Pretty Polly is rhapsodic – indeed, in the score Polly's numbers are entitled rhapsodies – and the 'passion chorales' sung by Punch's victims from their gibbet are gently ravishing.

In Birtwistle's only film score, for Sidney Lumet's *The Offence* (1972), he achieves something similar. Right at the start of the film, though we cannot understand what is happening, we see a police station on high alert after an officer (Sean Connery) has killed a man in interrogation and is now squaring up to his fellow officers. The sequence is in slow motion, and there is no dialogue. All we hear, apart from Birtwistle's score, are muffled sound effects. The electronic music, realised with the assistance of the composer's long-time collaborator Peter Zinovieff, contains some recognisable sounds – a low clarinet, a *staccato* muted trumpet, a child's or woman's voice – but mostly the music resembles a sonic cloud, full of foreboding as it slowly shapes and reshapes itself. It is rather beautiful in its lugubriousness, although above all, and like the film itself, it is intensely sad. These moments of melancholy lyricism are as typical of Birtwistle's music as the noisy blocks of sound and jagged rhythmic devices, though they tend to be eclipsed by them.

* * *

During a pre-concert talk in 1979 before the British premiere of his Sappho settings, ... *agm* ..., Birtwistle was asked about the influence of Stravinsky on his music, and also of Varèse and Messiaen. He replied simply that these figures and their music were influences on any composers 'worth their salt'. It was a perfectly fair and accurate answer, but the questioner had pinpointed three of the most important antecedents of this extremely original composer – from a structural point of view, perhaps the three most important. In *Earth Dances* their influences are keenly felt. The music contains big blocks of vivid, noisy sonority, such as Varèse employed in *Amériques*, and often enough they are articulated in terms of layers of pulse and metre that create complex, polymetric textures typical of Messiaen. Since *The Rite of Spring* was vitally important to both Varèse and Messiaen, it would not be wrong to think of Birtwistle as a third-generation Stravinskian, though this simplification presents nothing like the full picture of his music.

Still on the subject of influences, for example, there is the question of Birtwistle's 'Englishness', which is rather harder to pinpoint, let alone explain. It's partly to do with the melancholy hanging like a pall over the slow music in *Earth Dances* and elsewhere – a melancholy that can be found in English music at least as far back as the songs of John Dowland (a composer dear to Birtwistle), and arguably before that, in the music of the late-medieval composer John Dunstaple. There is also the fact that many of Birtwistle's pieces might best be heard as processions – the piece he composed soon after *Earth Dances* was a trumpet concerto entitled *Endless Parade* (1987) – and while this, too, might lead us back to *The Rite* (to the 'Procession of the Sage' and the 'Mystic Circles of the Young Girls'), it also leads us to a tradition that includes a series of slow movements from English music.

The musicologist Arnold Whittall once proposed a precursor to Birtwistle's music in a piece such as Gustav Holst's brooding little tone poem *Egdon Heath*, inspired by the nature writing in Thomas Hardy's novel *The Return of the Native*, but one might well add the slow movement – really a funeral march – of Elgar's second symphony and the desolate 'Epilogue' of Vaughan Williams's sixth. Notice that each of these examples of processional music is also another example of musical melancholy. In this same context, perhaps it is not entirely fanciful to mention the sombre march of Purcell's Music for the Funeral of Queen Mary. Asked by the music journalist Tom Service if he felt a part of this musical tradition, Birtwistle answered that it would be truer to say the tradition was part of him.

But another aspect of Englishness – from his own social background – might be thought to have found its way into this composer's music. Birtwistle was born in 1934 in Accrington, Lancashire, a quondam medieval hamlet lately grown into a dark hub of the industrial revolution. Like most such towns in Lancashire, it was cotton that led Accrington's economy in the nineteenth and early twentieth centuries – but if the world knows Accrington at all, it is probably for its bricks. The Empire State Building in New York is held up by foundations built from Accrington NORIs (NORI is 'iron' backwards), exceptionally hard bricks made of the fireclay found around the coal seams in Accrington's pits, and fired with that same coal. The truth is that, for all his musical antecedents, Birtwistle's music, too, has always seemed more dug up than written down, more quarried than composed, and *Earth Dances* is no exception. Its title, indeed, recalls Varèse's fascination with rocks and volcanoes as much as *The Rite of Spring*.

By the time he composed *Earth Dances*, Birtwistle had been dealing in extremes of register for more than twenty years, but seldom has this aspect of his music been more important structurally. The composer himself drew attention to the device, referring to six different 'strata' in the piece, which are defined by different musical materials, harmonic and rhythmic, as well as by the ranges of the instruments associated with them. For example, the lower-pitched instruments make use of the simplest of intervals, fourths and fifths, sometimes in parallel, creating a resonant sonority. The mid-range instruments play a lot of thirds, and in particular the note D rising to F, pitches that are important throughout the work and that create the sense of a tonal centre. These strata are seldom heard simultaneously, but in various smaller combinations, and their characteristic materials sometimes slip or rise to other strata via audible scale figures, as though the score were a gigantic Snakes and Ladders board. Birtwistle calls it a labyrinth.

Of course, one should not forget the second word of the title, for this music is full of dance patterns, and it is particularly in the play between the different strata that these dances occur. Indeed, it would be perfectly reasonable to read Birtwistle's title as the description of a continuing action, the word 'dances' as a verb: the earth *dances*.

There is lightness in this music, but that is not what we take away from it. All memories of the interlocking pulses and their resultant clockwork jigs are expunged by the final awful climax, a great piling up of sound leading to a fiercely ringing bell (the E below middle C). This gives way to octave Ds in the low strings – D, by now, has established itself as the tonal centre of *Earth Dances* – before the double basses' D finally sinks to C, the instrument's lowest note, fading from earshot as a rogue hi-hat cymbal continues to emit a wavering *staccato* pulse. According to Jonathan Cross in his sleeve note to Boulez's recording of the piece, 'It is as if we have returned to the depths of the earth, whence we came. This is a mystical experience of primordial power that puts us in touch both with nature and with unconscious feelings deep within ourselves.'

For all its earthy imagery, Birtwistle's piece, like all great music, has a purely musical logic. *Earth Dances* might be made from elemental sounds, from the primitive building blocks of music, but it is put together with evident skill, and above all with what Schoenberg (writing of Webern) called an 'absence of self-pity'. Even so, there is a lot of intuition involved in the process. In an interview with David Sylvester from 2001, Birtwistle explained: 'I say all the time that I've no idea what I'm doing, you know, because it's all about a sort of personal coherence . . . And whenever I have a solution to anything, it seems that I always want to walk away from it . . . I can only believe in the idea if it's a spontaneous thing . . .'

Now, it can be argued that most artists only find out what they are doing – and indeed what they *want* to do – by doing it. That is a common experience. Still, Birtwistle is an extreme example among composers. He seldom does much planning in advance of starting a piece, preferring to begin and then see where the ideas lead him. Once he is reasonably sure where the music is headed, once a piece is up and running, he will often destroy the first pages – the pages that led him to where he is. Perhaps he is covering his tracks.

When Birtwistle speaks of the process of composing, he often uses the analogy of a game, and certainly the Snakes and Ladders aspect of *Earth Dances* seems very much in that vein. I once suggested to him that, given the tendency of his music to brood and keen and erupt in hollow noise, this game of his was a rather melancholy one.

'Yes, but so's cricket,' he said. 'I think cricket's a very melancholy game.'

* * *

Birtwistle's interview with David Sylvester appears in the posthumously published *London Recordings*, a collection of the critic's interviews with artists of one sort or another – mostly visual artists. One of his more surprising interviewees is the former England cricket captain Mike (now Michael) Brearley. Sylvester and Brearley talk about art and sport, and about what an artist and a sportsman – specifically, a Test batsman facing a great fast bowler – might have in common.

'Uncompromisingness,' Brearley offers eventually, 'facing the facts, not turning one's face away, not giving up . . .'

It's a good answer, and it sums up the art of Harrison Birtwistle rather well, particularly the phrase 'not turning your face away'. But perhaps it also sums up most of the creative and performing artists mentioned in these pages. Perhaps, when artists confront the primitive side of their creativity, they too are 'facing the facts' and refusing to flinch. And perhaps that is why this aspect of our imaginations is – and always was – essential to the vitality of music and the other arts.

To borrow from Lévi-Strauss, artists are cooks. They take raw impulse and prepare it for consumption; composers transform sound into music. Perhaps the most striking sound in *Earth Dances* is, in fact, the most raw: that bell that comes just before the end.

Actually, it is a bell plate, and its ring is as hollow as the roar that had set the piece in motion more than half an hour earlier. The tone and timbre of the bell plate convey so much, and convey it directly. The percussionist executes a roll on the plate, making an extreme crescendo. It is arresting, because it represents a sudden solo voice in the piece, the bell emerging from the orchestra stark and unadorned. And then it rings on, beyond the control of the composer or the percussionist, the tone hanging in the air, gradually decaying in its own time. The bell plate's gleaming E pulls at the double basses' low D, but the D – as much drone as pedal point, as much tonic as drone – is bound to win because it exerts a gravitational pull over the music. Perhaps, in a piece called *Earth Dances*, this is only to be expected.

Alongside Jonathan Cross's words quoted above, we might set T.S. Eliot's lines from 'Little Gidding' in *Four Quartets* about the end of 'our exploring' being a return to where we began, knowing 'the place for the first time'. That is certainly how it feels at the end of *Earth Dances*. It is partly a function of the ritual cycles that make up Birtwistle's music. But it is also something to do with the raw sound of so much of this piece, and of that bell in particular. It is, above all, about renewal. When music goes in search of the primitive, it is always about renewal.

ACKNOWLEDGEMENTS

My first thanks must be to the six composers, Richard Barrett, Martin Bresnick, Karin Rehnqvist, Liza Lim, Pauline Oliveros and Brian Eno, who allowed me to interview them. The first part of Bresnick's interview (about Stravinsky) and the whole of the interview with Eno were originally broadcast on *The Music Show* on ABC Radio National, and my thanks, as ever, go to that program's producers, Maureen Cooney and Penny Lomax.

Sincere thanks to Michael Mason and Tony MacGregor at Radio National for commissioning the four-part companion series, *Earth Dances*.

Some of the words in the chapters 'Trying to Be Coarse', 'Dance of the Earth' and 'The Sound of Skin' first appeared in essays for the *Australian Financial Review*. My grateful acknowledgement to Robert Bolton for commissioning them.

Alan Lamb's words in 'Droning On' are from my radio series *Dots on the Landscape*, produced by Maureen Cooney and first broadcast on ABC Classic FM in 2001.

Thanks to Maria Carlson for permission to quote her translation of Aleksandr Blok's 'The Twelve' (Kansas University ScholarWorks: http://hdl.handle.net/1808/6598).

For practical assistance, conversations wide and narrow,

suggestions large and small, I thank John Addison, Shirley Apthorp, Leanne Bear, Murray Black, Austin Buckett, Peter Byles, Nick Byrne, Stefan Cassomenos, Simon Charles, Matthew Coorey, Samuel Curckpatrick, Peter Dasent, Robert Davidson, Julian Day, Graham Devlin, Roma Dix, Michael Dunn, John Encarnacao, Kate Fagan, Diana Ford, Christopher Fox, Yvonne Frindle, James Gavin, Sam Gillies, Paul Gough, Iain Grandage, Dave Graney, Andrée Greenwell, Anthony Heinrichs, Moya Henderson, Michael Hooper, Chris Howlett, Ione, Peter Ireland, Luke Jaaniste, Rob Keeley, Albert Landa, Somaya Langley, Siobhan Lenihan, Noemi Liba, Anthony Linden-Jones, Danny Maratos, Christine McCombe, Tabatha McFadyen, Marshall McGuire, Gretchen Miller, Richard Miller, Ian Mitchell, Kate Moore, Lisa Moore, Jeff Mueller, Ian Munro, John Napier, Nguyên Vaň Anh, Nguyên Vaň Đô, Colin Offord, Cathy Peters, Vincent Plush, Aleks Pusz, Tim Pye, Ben Quilty, Brian Ritchie, Phil Slater, Russell Stapleton, Cathy Strickland, Angela Turner, Gemma Turner, Liam Viney, Võ Thành Đình, Andy Vores, Kim Waldock, Belinda Webster, Jessica Wells and Martin Wesley-Smith.

My biggest thanks must go to Chris Feik at Black Inc., for this book was his idea; to Julian Welch for his sensitive editing; to my researcher, Angharad Davis, who dug up things I would never have found (nor known where to find); and to my wife, Anni Heino – always my first and best reader.

I would also like to mention my daughter, Elsie. Usually when she is nearby whacking a drum I find it hard to work, but with this book, the whacking suggested some fruitful lines of enquiry.

Bibliography

Albright, Daniel, *Untwisting the Serpent: Modernism in music, literature, and other arts* (Chicago: University of Chicago Press, 2000).

Beard, David, *Harrison Birtwistle's Operas and Music Theatre* (Cambridge: Cambridge University Press, 2012).

Bloechl, Olivia A., *Native American Song at the Frontiers of Early Modern Music* (Cambridge: Cambridge University Press, 2008).

Buzacott, Martin & Andrew Ford, *Speaking in Tongues: The songs of Van Morrison* (Sydney: ABC Books, 2005).

Coulombe, Renée T., 'The Insatiable Banshee: Voracious vocalizing . . . riot grrl . . . and the blues', in *Audible Traces: Gender, identity, and music*, ed. Elaine Barkin and Lydia Hamessley (Zürich; Los Angeles: Carciofoli, 1999).

Cross, Ian, 'Music and Biocultural Evolution' in *The Cultural Study of Music: A critical introduction*, ed. Martin Clayton, Trevor Herbert and Richard Middleton (New York: Routledge, 2003).

Crouch, Stanley, *Considering Genius: Writings on jazz* (New York: Basic Civitas Books, 2006).

Dean, Matt, *The Drum: A history* (Lanham: Scarecrow Press, 2012).

Downes, Julia, 'The Expansion of Punk Rock: Riot grrrl challenges to gender power relations in British indie music subcultures', in *Women's Studies*, 41 (2012).

Dylan, Bob, *Chronicles: Volume one* (New York: Simon & Schuster, 2004).

Encarnacao, John, *Punk Aesthetics and New Folk: Down the old plank road* (Farnham: Ashgate, 2014).

Fillion, Michelle, 'Beethoven's Mass in C and the Search for Inner Peace' in *Beethoven Forum Vol 7*, ed. Mark Evan Bonds & Elaine Sisman (Lincoln: University of Nebraska Press, 1999).

Fisk, Josiah, ed., *Composers on Music: Eight centuries of writings* (Boston: Northeastern University Press, 2nd edition, 1997).

Ford, Andrew, *Composer to Composer: Conversations about contemporary music* (St Leonards: Allen & Unwin, 1993).

——, *Illegal Harmonies: Music in the modern age* (Collingwood: Black Inc., 3rd edition, 2011).

Freud, Sigmund & Josef Breuer, trans. Nicola Luckhurst, *Studies on Hysteria* (*Studien über Hysterie*, 1895) (London: Penguin, 2004).

Gavin, James, *Intimate Nights: The golden age of New York cabaret* (New York: Back Stage Books, 2006).

Givan, Benjamin, 'Thelonious Monk's Pianism' in *The Journal of Musicology*, 26, no. 3 (2009).

Hall, Michael, *Harrison Birtwistle* (London: Robson Books, 1984).

——, *Harrison Birtwistle in Recent Years* (London: Robson Books, 1998).

Harvey, Jonathan, ed. Michael Downes, *Music and Inspiration* (London: Faber, 1999).

Kandinsky, Wassily, trans. M.T. Sadler, *Concerning the Spiritual in Art* (*Über das Geistiger in der Kunst*, 1911) (London: Tate Gallery Publishing, 2006).

Kelley, Robin D.G., *Thelonious Monk: The life and times of an American original* (New York: Free Press, 2009).

Larkin, Philip, *All What Jazz: A record diary 1961–1971* (London: Faber, rev. ed. 1985).

Leonard, Marion, *Gender in the Music Industry: Rock, discourse and girl power* (Aldershot: Ashgate, 2007).

Lévi-Strauss, Claude, trans. John and Doreen Weightman, *The Raw and the Cooked* (*Le Cru et le cuit*, 1964) (New York: Octagon Books, 1970).

Maddocks, Fiona, *Harrison Birtwistle: Wild Tracks, a conversation diary* (London: Faber, 2014).

Mellers, Wilfrid, ed. John Paynter, *Between Old Worlds and New: Occasional writings on music* (London: Cygnus Arts, 1997).

Mellers, Wilfrid, *Caliban Reborn: Renewal in twentieth-century music* (New York: Harper & Row, 1967).

——, *Singing in the Wilderness: Music and ecology in the twentieth century* (Urbana: University of Illinois Press, 2001).

——, *The Masks of Orpheus: Seven stages in the story of European music* (Manchester: University of Manchester Press, 1987).

Napier, A. David, *Foreign Bodies: Performance, art, and symbolic anthropology* (Berkeley: University of California Press, 1992).

Nyman, Michael, *Experimental Music: Cage and beyond* (Cambridge: Cambridge University Press, 1974, 2nd edition 1999).

O'Brian, Patrick, *Picasso* (Glasgow: William Collins, 1976).

Potter, John, *Vocal Authority: Singing style and ideology* (Cambridge: Cambridge University Press, 1998).

Rhodes, Colin, *Primitivism and Modern Art* (London: Thames & Hudson, 1994).

Ross, Alex, *The Rest Is Noise: Listening to the twentieth century* (New York: Farrar, Straus and Giroux, 2007).

Schoenberg, Arnold, trans. Roy E. Carter, *Theory of Harmony* (*Harmonielehre*, 1911) (Berkeley: University of California Press, 1978).

Solomon, Maynard, *Late Beethoven: Music, thought, imagination* (Berkeley: University of California Press, 2003).

Sylvester, David, *Interviews with Francis Bacon* (enlarged 3rd ed. of *The Brutality of Fact*) (London: Thames & Hudson, 1993).

——, *London Recordings* (London: Chatto & Windus, 2003).

Taruskin, Richard, *Stravinsky and the Russian Traditions: A biography of the works through Mavra* (Berkeley: University of California Press, 1996).

Thwaites, Penelope, ed., *The New Percy Grainger Companion* (Woodbridge: The Boydell Press, 2010).

Toop, David, *Ocean of Sound: Aether talk, ambient sound and imaginary worlds* (London: Serpent's Tail, 1995).

Torgovnick, Marianna, *Gone Primitive: Savage intellects, modern lives* (Chicago: University of Chicago Press, 1991).

van der Bliek, Rob, ed., *The Thelonious Monk Reader* (Oxford: Oxford University Press, 2001).

Weininger, Otto, trans. Ladislaus Löb, ed. Daniel Steuer & Laura Marcus, *Sex and Character: An investigation of fundamental principles* (*Geschlecht und Charakterr: Eine prinzipielle Untersuchung*, 1903) (Bloomington: Indiana University Press, 2005).

INDEX